Mechanics of ...

MW01146021

ISBN 9781479110179
LCCN 2012914984
CreateSpace Independent Publishing Platform
North Charleston, SC

SUDDENLY

and

UNEXPECTEDLY

NON-FICTION

UNPRECEDENTED – CERTAIN – IMMINENT – IRREVERSIBLE

THE END OF OUR TIMES

by

T. Michael Fahy

Cover Design by Barbara Canning Martin

Published by
The Center for the Divine Will
P.O. Box 415 - Jacksboro, TN 37757– USA

CONTENTS

Prefatory Remarks
For Every Reader

This book was originally intended for a limited audience. As it was being written it seemed that it should be for all peoples, because all peoples will soon be vitally affected by what is made known herein. Some people will quickly grasp what is contained in these pages. Others will have to struggle with some of the words, terms, and the very serious and unprecedented realities described herein.

For the past 42 years the author has been heavily involved in the subject matter of the realities found in this book; and by invitation has travelled the world over to assist others in preparing for the horrific end of these times and especially for the happy new times to follow.

There are many books, magazines and videos about the events that took place in a tiny mountain village named San Sebastian in the early to mid-1960's. Even though several million people from all over the world have read or heard about those happenings at one time or another, most who are still alive, are not aware that the time is now very close at hand for the unfolding of the unprecedented, catastrophic events so strangely and wonderfully made known at San Sebastian. It seems that the majority of those few who are aware and preparing are sometimes confused about the sequence of these coming events.

The purpose of *"Suddenly and Unexpectedly,"* is not to give a full account of the vast material available about those events or the correlated manifestations of Divine Mercy and Justice, but to present an authentic, compelling, non-speculative and non-fictional account of the rapidly approaching, and gravely serious events, made known in advance at San Sebastian, that have no precedent in human history, and their temporal and eternal conse- quences for all people on earth, about which almost the totality of the human race is completely oblivious even by those who are warning others about pending economic, social, military and natural disasters.

And then, the purpose of this book is to introduce to those, who do not yet know, secrets never before known until now about the prodigies, delights, joys, extraordinary blessings and permanent happiness of life in the renewed world that will happily follow the present and coming, terrible upheavals, revolutions, disasters, and sufferings.

Chapter One
"The Nights of Screams"

10:30 PM, June 19 and 10:30 PM, June 20, 1962— The village of San Sebastian in the mountains of northern Spain.

Key persons: Four young villagers, a Catholic Priest, and two very distinctive other persons. What happened among them in 1962 will very soon have incalculable consequences for all peoples in all places on earth.

In 1962, the little village of San Sebastian had 60 to 70 stone houses and about 300 inhabitants, no electricity or running water, no cars, no paved streets or sidewalks, and only one telephone. In the cold weather, heat came from fireplaces, stoves, and from farm animals stabled next to or beneath the living area of

1

some homes. The generally pious and contented people were mostly shepherds, cattle raisers, farmers and domestics; and there was at least one stone mason.

Very strange and astonishing things had been happening in the village of San Sebastian, beginning the prior year on June 18, 1961. Most of these exceptional things that had been taking place during the past year were very beautiful, charming and edifying, others were quite serious and foreboding, but nothing yet had happened like the events that took place on the two nights of June 19 and 20 of 1962. Interestingly, what began to happen in this village in 1961 was directly linked to something very extraordinary that had occurred 44 years earlier in central Portugal on the 13th of October 1917. This linkage will be explained later, but for now let us focus on the "nights of the screams" in the village of San Sebastian and what it means for those living today.

On the *first night of the screams*, June 19, 1962, thirteen-year-old girls, Mari Loli Mazon and Jacinta Gonzalez, and twelve-year-old Mary Cruz Gonzalez arrived in the dark of the night at the appointed spot in the "calleja"—a sunken, rocky lane that ascended moderately upward from the mountain village to the base of a bluff on top of which was a grouping of nine, large pine trees. Their friend, thirteen-year-old Concepción Gonzales (Conchita) hadn't come with them as expected. Her mother made her stay home because she had injured her knee earlier that day. But there was a large number of villagers and visitors from other places—a few hundred in total—who followed the young girls to the designated location in the "calleja," next to the school teacher's property with the now famous apple tree.

The atmosphere among the people was curious and expectant. What was supposed to happen? Why had these girls been instructed to come to this spot so late at night? Who had instructed them? and why had the girls been told to tell the people that they were not to follow them should they leave the appointed spot and disappear into the darkness of that night?

Then suddenly and irresistibly at precisely 10:30 PM, Mari Loli and Jacinta moved quickly away from the crowd and further into the darkness, up the "calleja" and out-of-sight of the people who remained at the designated spot as they had been instructed. Young Mary Cruz seems to have remained behind that night. (Note: Some sources say that Mary Cruz did not participate in what was about to occur. Others believe that she did.)

Then, without any forewarning, horrifying screams and anguished wails were heard coming from the two young girls, Mari Loli and Jacinta. Their cries and screams went on for 50 minutes! Some of the terrified people who had remained at the designated spot thought it had to do with the end of the world. The girls were heard to cry out: *"Stop telling us those things!" Wait! Wait! . . . Everyone should confess! They should get ready! Oh! Oh!"*

At one point the girls came back down the "calleja" toward the people, arriving closely enough that the people could see the girls facing back toward the place they had been. At least one of the girls was seen thrusting her arms forward as if attempting to push away something terrible and dangerous. The screams and agonizing wails continued for some time and finally came to a stop.

When this terrifying encounter concluded, the shaken villagers returned to their homes, and the equally frightened visitors returned to their vehicles or to the rooms which some of the villagers had provided for them in their homes. It was a restless night for most, but the next night would be much worse. On that next night the people wouldn't return to their homes or to their rooms or to their vehicles—at least until many hours later, after the sunrise.

Due to their emotional state, with tear-stained faces and their incoherent speech, the two thirteen-year-old girls, Mari Loli Mazon and Jacinta Gonzalez were unable to respond to questions of the people except to say, *"We must return tomorrow at the same time."* They then went straight to the little cafe owned by Mari Loli's father, Ceferino, and wrote and signed a statement dated, June 19, 1962, based on the horrifying things they had seen and heard that night which had caused them to scream so pitifully. This hurried statement of their experience was minimal at best, but years later, in interviews by certain priests and laity, they would disclose much more. *(That written statement and the other serious disclosures will be presented in the next chapter along with the incredible facts about what they saw and heard, and who or what was giving them orders.)*

Conchita Gonzalez, who had stayed at home in obedience to her mother, had her own but different experience at the same time that Mari Loli and Jacinta were having theirs in the "calleja." From within her own house Conchita was very much aware of the events and the screams taking place with the other two girls in the "calleja," and she told this to those people who were with her at her home because they were unaware of the screams. In her own experience while holding a sheet of paper up in the air with one hand and writing things on it with the other, Conchita did not scream, but she did exclaim, ***"Ah, that is why Loli and Jacinta are crying at this present moment! Oh! How sad it is; I will not write that..."***

All three girls would be together in the "calleja" the next night, however; and what they would experience the next night would be worse and even more frightening.

(Mari Cruz was involved with the other girls in the strange happenings of the prior twelve months and to a lesser degree afterwards. It is uncertain wether she participated directly in the frightening events of either night. The information available about Mari Cruz's involvement on both nights of the screams is sketchy.)

Indeed, the *second night of screams*, June 20, 1962 was even more frightening than the first. It would last three and a half hours. On this night Conchita joined Mari Loli and Jacinta as they arrived at the same designated spot as before, in the "calleja," at 10:30 PM. Again, a crowd had gathered there but the numbers were smaller than the night before. It was the eve of the Feast of Corpus Christi and there was a new observer this night—Fr. Felix Larrazábal, a Franciscan priest, stationed in Santander about 50 miles away.

All three girls moved away from the crowd up the "calleja" and out of sight. Then suddenly, like the night before, the people heard cries and screams so terrifying that their effect was more powerful upon the people than the first night of screams. A number of people testified that their knees buckled and shook from fright. One of these persons with the shaking knees was the stone mason, Pepe Diaz—a rugged man who had often walked calmly at night through the fields inhabited by wolves that extended from the village throughout the mountainous terrain.

The girls' cries were so pitiful that several people felt like running to the children to save them or help them. The priest, Fr. Larrazábal, actually began to run to the girls but was stopped by Ceferino Mazon, who said to the priest, *"Here, we are all equal,"* in remembrance of the orders that none of the people were to follow the girls.

The people, including the men, were so frightened that they begged the priest, *"Pray, Father, Pray!"* And he began to pray. And as they all prayed, the screams of the girls subsided, even though they were too far away to hear the prayers. But when the prayers stopped, the screams became even louder and more terrifying. The screams did not sound like those of teenage girls, but were strange and exceedingly frightening. When the prayers resumed, the agonizing wails subsided as before.

The people heard the girls cry out, ***"Oh! Don't let this happen; don't let this come. . . May everyone go to confession first! Forgive us! Don't let this happen!. . .***

The people were crying and moaning. They could even feel the fright of the girls who had extended their hands up in front of themselves as if they were trying to push something away. And among the people, all could feel the fright within one another.

Pepe Diaz, the stone mason, heard Mari Loli cry out, *"Wait, wait. Take the little children first. Give everyone a chance to confess!. . ."* He said that all were terrorized with a fear that they could not put into words but kept inside themselves.

Finally, after three and a half hours, the great drama of that night in the village of San Sebastian took a turn towards quietude, but no one went back home or to their vehicles. That is, except for Conchita's aunt, Maximina Gonzalez, who ran rapidly back to her home. She was so shaken by what had happened that she was convinced that the heavens were about to fall upon the earth. For her, this was the last day. She was even about to confess her sins publicly, because she had the feeling that this was the end of the world. She was thinking about her father, an old man, about whom she was reproaching herself for her behavior at times. And as soon as the girls returned to normal, Maximina ran home to see him. He was in bed, and she told him, *"Father, forgive me! This is the end of the world!."* Then she returned to the "calleja" and rejoined the people.

Suddenly and Unexpectedly

The reason for her words was accentuated by what the girls said when the things they had just seen had stopped, and they had returned to a more normal state. Some people questioned the girls and they said, *"We have seen the Chastisement; we have seen something worse than if we were being burned alive. It is going to be something horrible. . . horrible!"* (Much more on this is in Chapter six.)

It was now 2:00 AM. Everyone was so emotionally involved in what had taken place, especially the three girls who had been so involved in the terrifying mysteries of that night that caused them to scream so loudly and cry with so much anguish, that no one wanted to go home but felt impelled to remain together in the "calleja" and pray, pray pray! The dread of some unknown, all consuming and imminent catastrophe of the greatest magnitude was shared by all. They felt the overwhelming need of one another's support, the need of repentance, great sorrow for their sins, and an irresistible desire to beg the mercy of God—some with tears in their eyes.

At 6:00 AM there was a beautiful sunrise. It was now June 21st, Feast of Corpus Christi. Everyone followed Fr. Larrazábal. down to the Church and all went to confession to him except one or two persons. The confessions were made with great sincerity and repentance. Then Fr. Larrazábal offered Mass and the people received Holy Communion with great respect and devotion.

Chapter Two

The Awesome

In June 1961, one year before the *nights of the screams*, very unusual things began to happen in this village known as San Sebastian de Garabandal, but simply called Garabandal by most outsiders. The addition of the word, *Garabandal*, to the name of the village serves to distinguish it from other Spanish villages named after Saint Sebastian and relates to the mountain named *Garabandal* on the north side of this village.

It all began in the late afternoon of Sunday, June 18, 1961. The more mature village children typically gathered on Sunday afternoons in an open area of the village close to the church to entertain themselves in whatever ways that interested them. Suddenly, twelve-year-old Conchita Gonzalez got the exciting but mischievous idea to go pick some apples in the school teacher's yard and whispered to her friend, Mary Cruz Gonzalez, age eleven, to join her, which she did. One thing led to another, and before long Mari Loli Mazon and Jacinta Gonzalez, both twelve-years-old that year, joined them in picking unripened apples from the one apple tree in the school teacher's yard, next to the "calleja."

(The three girls with the last names of Gonzalez were not closely related.)

When they realized that the school teacher was at home and seemed to notice something irregular going on at the apple tree, the four girls quickly climbed over a low part of the stone wall that separated the teacher's yard from the "calleja." They moved up the "calleja" somewhat, then sat on the stony ground and began to eat their stolen, unripe apples.

Suddenly they were startled by a loud noise similar to a clap of thunder, which frightened them. Then all four girls felt a pang of conscience about their escapade in the school teacher's yard and the apples they had taken without permission. They started throwing stones to their left to chase away the devil whom they felt must have tempted them. After a few minutes they felt better and started playing a type of game of marbles with little stones they found in the "calleja."

Then, once again, something happened with unexpected suddenness. Conchita was heard by the other three girls making a strange sound. They noticed an unusual look on her face as she was staring in a fixed direction. Her complexion seemed to pale. Her guttural sounds made Mari Loli, Jacinta and Mary Cruz believe that Conchita was sick. They immediately turned to run to the village and get some adult help. But, as they turned in the direction that Conchita was staring, they, too, froze in their places. They were seeing the same thing that Conchita was seeing! What they saw was strikingly beautiful with a shining brilliance that didn't dazzle their eyes. It was an Angel who looked at them but did not say a word and soon disappeared.

The girls became quite emotional and they rushed to the Church. People noticed their unusual behavior; then one by one they spoke to different persons about what happened that early evening of June 18, 1961. The fine details of what happened the remainder of that night in the village are described in several books on Garabandal.

The four girls decided to go back to the "calleja" the following evening at 8:30 PM, June 19, 1961. They said prayers and waited, but the Angel did not come. Conchita went to bed a little before ten o'clock but was restless and unable to sleep, so she began to pray. Then she heard a voice that said, *"Don't be troubled; you will see me again."* The next day, Conchita found out from the other three girls that they had also heard a voice telling them not to worry and that they would see him again.

The evening of June 20th found all four girls back in the "calleja," although Conchita's mother was reluctant to let her go at first. Their hopes were fulfilled when the Angel came and appeared to them. Again, he did not say anything, but this time things were different. The girls found themselves surrounded by light, unable to see beyond the light. This strange experience caused them to scream for a moment. When the Angel left, the light surrounding them disappeared and the girls were startled to realize that they were in darkness. It was 9:30 PM.

On June 21st, after school and after having completed their chores, the four girls returned to the "calleja." This time there were some witnesses to what happened. The Angel appeared again this night, and, following instructions from the parish priest, the girls asked him who he was and why he had come. But they got no answer. The girls were on their knees upon the rocks. Their heads were turned upward and their eyes were riveted toward the Angel. Their faces took on a beautiful aspect attracting the admiring attention of the onlookers. The four children were in a state of ecstasy. The witnesses were very excited and emotional due to what they were observing, although only the four girls could see the Angel. This excitement was contagious and soon spread throughout the village and then to neigboring villages and beyond.

The Angel's visitation on June 21st came to an end, but he returned on June 22nd and the following three nights. On June 26th and June 27th the Angel did not appear nor did he appear on June 29th or June 30th. Nor did he speak to the girls at anytime during his appearances in June of 1961, though he usually smiled—and sometimes a lot.

Finally, on July 1, 1961, he spoke for the first time! This was his ninth appearance to date, although he had not spoken before, there was some mysterious writing that had been seen beneath the Angel when he appeared, which the girls did not understand. One of the girls remembered the first two words of the first line, which were *"There must."* Another girl remembered that the last line had some capital letters, *"XVIII MCMLXI,"* but did not know what they meant until someone explained that the letters were Roman Numerals.

Before going further with this story about the Angel's visit on July 1, 1961, let us describe the Angel (who on the following day was identified as St. Michael the Archangel) as the four girls of Garabandal came to understand. The young village girls said that he appeared as a boy of roughly nine years of age, but conveyed a presence of great strength and importance.

Suddenly and Unexpectedly

"He was dressed in a long flowing blue tunic without a belt. His wings are rather long, very lovely, pink in color. His face was neither long nor round; his nose was handsome; his eyes dark; and the face tan. His hands were fine with short nails; his feet weren't seen." [This description was much different from the appearance of the statue of St. Michael the Archangel in the village church.]

Here are some passages from Old and New Testaments concerning the Archangel Michael:

The Book of Daniel: Chapter 12, verse 1:

At that time shall arise Michael, the great prince who has charge of your people.

And there shall be a time of trouble, such as never has been since there was a nation

till that time; but at that time your people shall be delivered, every one whose name shall be found written in the book.

Matthew: Chapter 24, verses 21-22:

For then there will be great tribulation, such as has not been from the beginning of the world until now, no, and never will be.

And if those days had not been shortened, no human being would be saved; but for the sake of the elect those days will be shortened.

[These two verses from Matthew seem to correlate with Daniel 12:1.]

Non-Fiction

Apocalypse: Chapter 12, verses 7-12:

Now war arose in heaven, Michael and his angels fighting against the dragon; and the dragon and his angels fought, but they were defeated and there was no longer any place for them in heaven.

And the great dragon was thrown down, that ancient serpent, who is called the Devil and Satan, the deceiver of the whole world—he was thrown down to the earth, and his angels were thrown down with him.

And I heard a loud voice in heaven, saying, "Now the salvation and the power and the kingdom of our God and the authority of his Christ have come, for the accuser of our brethren has been thrown down, who accuses them day and night before our God.

And they have conquered him by the blood of the Lamb and by the word of their testimony, for they loved not their lives even unto death.

Rejoice then, O heaven and you that dwell therein! But woe to you, O earth and sea, for the devil has come down to you in great wrath, because he knows that his time is short!"

Suddenly and Unexpectedly

The above passages will become quite relevant in later chapters.

The Angel had something special to say to the four young girls. It was Saturday, July 1, 1961, and He said to them:

"I come to announce to you a visit by the Virgin under the title of Our Lady of Mount Carmel, who will appear to you tomorrow, Sunday."

Full of joy and excitement, all four girls responded with: *"Let her come right away!"* The Angel smiled.

Now, the reasons for his many visits were becoming clear. The Angel was preparing the way for the Queen of Heaven—the spiritual Mother of humanity, who had given us the Messiah and Redeemer, for He had given Her to us as Mother while dying on the Cross at Calvary with his words to St. John the Evangelist, *"Behold thy Mother."*

The four girls of Garabandal began to speak to the Angel and ask many questions; and he was quite willing to converse at length. They talked a lot about the many things that had happened over the last thirteen days, beginning on that late afternoon on June 18th. When they asked him about the mysterious writing that had appeared beneath him, he answered: *"The Virgin will tell you about it."*

The encounter lasted two hours. The Angel's last words that night were: *"I will come tomorrow with the Virgin."*

July 2, 1961, the Mother of Jesus Arrives from Heaven. Her visitation begins on the Catholic feast day of the biblical Visitation of Mary to Elizabeth, Mother of John the Baptist [Church calendar at that time]. During her series of visitations at Garabandal, She was only visible to the four girls and one priest, but She had much to do in San Sebastian de Garabandal and had things of exceedingly grave importance to tell all humanity through the four young girls. She let us know the sequence of events, unprecedented in human history, which will bring about the *"End of the Times"* (not the end of the world). She told us what must be done as She knew the fate of all humanity is at stake, just as in the days of Noah.

The village became very crowded that day. Present among the multitude were members of the civil guard, several priests and doctors.

It was just before 6:00 PM, when the four girls were making their way up the "calleja" that they suddenly exclaimed, *"The Virgin!"* (See note at end of this chapter.)

The Mother of Jesus, sent by God, appeared at San Sebastian de Garabandal with an Angel on each side.

Suddenly and Unexpectedly

She told the girls that one of these was St. Michael. The girls did not seem to recognize the other Angel who was dressed like St. Michael and looked almost identical. Years later, Jacinta, said that she was very sure that the other Angel was St. Gabriel.

A little while into this marvelous encounter, Conchita was heard to say, *Oh! What an eye!"* To the right of one of the Angels and about the height of the Virgin, the girls saw an eye of great size. Some witnesses said that the girls had tears in their eyes and looked very pale. It seems that this scene represented the all-seeing Eye of God. It was within a triangle. The triangle, itself, was within a square of red flames of fire, and there was some writing associated with the eye.

During this rather lengthy visit of the Lady from Heaven the four girls had very relaxed and familiar conversation with Her. They told the Lady all sorts of things they had been doing in their village lives. The Lady smiled at their words. She was dressed in a white robe with a blue mantle and wore a crown of golden stars. She seemed to be about 17 or 18 years old.

A description of the Lady from Heaven is found in Conchita's diary: *"The Virgin comes in a white cloak, a blue mantel, a crown of little golden stars. The feet are not seen; the hands are open and there is a scapular hanging from the right hand: the scapular is brown. Her hair is long, a dark chestnut brown color, wavy, parted in the middle; the face somewhat elongated; the nose also somewhat long, and fine; the mouth, very beautiful with lips a little full; the color of her face tan, much lighter than that of the angel, different. The voice, very beautiful, a voice very unusual. I don't know how to explain it. There is no other woman who resembles the Virgin, either in the voice or in anything. Sometimes she carries the Baby in her arms. He is very small, like a newborn baby with a round face the same color as the Virgin's. He has a very small mouth, and hair slightly long. He is dressed in something like a blue tunic."*

This appearance of Our Lady of Mount Carmel de Garabandal would be the first of approximately 2,000 visits. Her last visit would be on November 13, 1965. So many marvelous things happened during those years in Garabandal that even the many publications and videos on the subject do not convey it all. Pope Paul VI referred to what happened during those years with these words: *"It is the most beautiful story of humanity since the days of Christ. It is like a second life of the Virgin on earth. And we can never be grateful enough for it."*

Speaking of Pope Paul VI, it should be noted that in 1966, when Conchita, then 17 years old, was called to Rome by Cardinal Ottaviani, the Pope met her and those with her and said to her, *"Conchita, I bless you and with me the whole Church blesses you."*

From this point forward, in this chapter, a list of various happenings during the first year will be cited and then, in Chapter Four will come the story and descriptions of the "Awful" which were of so great a concern to the Lady from Heaven who so much loves the children of our Father. Readers must take heed because there is truly, very little time left.

The Beautiful Lady from Heaven returned the following day, July 3rd, appearing to the four girls from 7:30 to 8:00 in the evening.

On July 4, 1961, a Tuesday, the Virgin appeared smiling, and her first words to the girls were: *"Do you know the meaning ot the writing that the angel carried beneath him?"*

The girls replied in unison, *"No, we don't know."*

And the Lady from Heaven told them: *"It gives a message that I am going to explain to you so that you can tell it to the people on the 18th of October."* Then She gave it to them, and they kept it secret until that day in October.

Non-Fiction

The days leading up to October 18th, were full of activity between Heaven and the piece of earth called San Sebastian de Garabandal. The Virgin Queen of Heaven began to make her appearances almost daily, especially at the grouping of nine, large pine trees at the summit of the bluff above the "calleja." But She also began to lead the girls, not always all four at the same time, to every room of every dwelling in the village, giving instructions to the girls about applying the sign of the cross with their small crucifixes to every bed in the homes. In this manner the Virgin Mary gave her blessings to these homes which very likely included graces to help the married members be faithful to the vows and divine precepts proper to marriage. There were times when She brought Jesus as a Baby in her arms. The Archangel Michael also was very much involved and frequently brought sacramental Eucharistic Hosts to some of the girls on days when no priest was available in the village. He obtained the consecrated Hosts from tabernacles on earth.

On July 23rd the girls began to witness a series of cosmic phenomena. The girls saw large stars with long tails, and sometimes these cosmic phenomena were seen by everyone there.

Friday and Saturday of July 28 and 29, 1961 came to be known as the *"Two Evenings of Tears,"* in which Mari Loli and Jacinta were shown the sorrowful scene of

Suddenly and Unexpectedly

"The Cup filling up with the wine of the Wrath of God." The Virgin spoke to them of the trials and sins of humanity and the consequences that lay ahead. For those of good will and born in the 1940's and earlier, the consequences of the enormous sins of the past 50 years are obvious and will become far graver still.

About 400 people were present on the second night of the tears, July 29, 1961. Among them were two brothers, and both were Catholic priests. One was Luis and the other was Ramon. Their surnames were Andreu. They belonged to the Jesuit order and both had doctorates in theology. The presence of Fr. Luis Andreu was especially significant, as he would soon become a truly exceptional witness, in a very extraordinary way. These two nights of tears involved Mari Loli and Jacinta.

The night of August 8–9, 1961 would bring great attention to the 36-year-old Jesuit priest, Fr. Luis Andreu. On the August 8, Fr. Luis came to Garabandal for his third visit and had been asked by the pastor to take over the pastoral duties that day. Fr. Luis offered Mass in a noticeably admirable manner that morning. At 2:11 in the afternoon, all four girls had a visitation from the Lady who had come from Heaven, and as usual, the young girls went into an ecstasy, seeing no one but the Great Lady and one another. Fr. Luis was present and took notes as he watched the conversations between the girls and the Celestial Virgin. He was very intent, and at times tears were seen running down his cheeks. The Virgin left for Heaven at 3:00 PM, and the ecstasy of the girls also ended. However, during the ecstasy observers heard some words indicating that there might be another visit of the beautiful Lady that night, it and would last for two hours. And so it happened. The visitation of the Queen of Heaven began in the Church at 9:00 PM with the corresponding ecstasy of the four girls of Garabandal. At 9:40 PM, remaining in ecstasy, the girls followed the Mother of Jesus who led them all the way up to the now famous group of pines above the village. Fr. Luis followed the girls all the way and took a position near them where they had knelt down. He was watching them very closely. . .

Then, the people, who had crowded around, noticed that Fr. Luis seemed to suddenly become overwhelmed with emotion, and he cried out loudly: *"Miracle! Miracle! Miracle! Miracle!"* The girls saw him during their ecstasy and were surprised because they had never seen anyone besides themselves and the Lady from Heaven while in these ecstasies. The Virgin told them that he was seeing Her and the Miracle. The Miracle that Fr. Luis saw that night was the one that the Virgin had spoken about to the girls. Fr. Luis saw in advance the Great Miracle that God will work at Garabandal on a future Thursday night at 8:30 PM that will have immense effects upon the human society that will have survived what the girls would see the following

June on the first night of the screams, mentioned in Chapter One. The subject of the Great Miracle will be detailed in Chapter Six of this book.

At 10:00 PM, Fr. Luis Andreu returned to normal, and the girls, still in ecstasy, began their descent (a rapid one in spite of the treacherous way down) to the Church. Late at night Fr. Luis was given a ride in a jeep to the bottom of the mountain arriving in the village of Cosio. The pastor of Cosio and Garabandal, Fr. Valentin Marichalar, came up to the jeep to greet Fr. Luis, who looked at him with seriousness and with a clear voice said, *"Fr. Valentin, what the girls say is true; but don't repeat around here what I am telling you now. The Church should use great prudence in these matters."*

In Cosio, Fr. Luis changed to another vehicle, owned by one of the members of the group who were returning to Aguilar del Campoo by way of Torrelavega and Reinosa. On the way to Torrelavega, Fr. Luis spoke several times, saying: *"What a gift the Virgin has given me! I can't have the least doubt about the truth of what is happening to the girls."*

After leaving Torrelavega, Fr. Luis slept for almost an hour, awakening before arrival in Reinosa. He remarked to his fellow passengers, *"I've slept very well, and I am in good shape! I feel great. I'm not even tired."*

Non-Fiction

At about 4:00 in the morning of August 9, 1961, the travelers stopped for a drink of water at a fountain. Then resuming their drive toward Reinosa, which was close, Fr. Luis continued his words about his experience in Garabandal at the pines. He said, *"I feel myself truly full of joy and happiness. What a gift the Virgin has given me. How fortunate to have a mother like her in Heaven! We shouldn't have any fear of the supernatural life. We should learn to act toward the Virgin as the children do. They have given us an example. I can't have the least doubt about the truth of their visions. . . Why has the most Holy Virgin chosen us!?. . . Today is the happiest day of my life."*

With that he stopped speaking. One of the persons in the car asked him something. Getting no answer, that person asked him if something was wrong. Fr. Luis simply said, *"No, nothing. I am sleeping."* Then he leaned his head forward, making a soft sound in his throat and died!! He was 36-years-old and in excellent health! [Fr. Luis Andreau had died of joy!]

His funeral took place in Oña in the district of Burgos. A few days later he would speak to the girls of Garabandal from Heaven.

Fr. Luis died at 4:20 AM on Wednesday, August 9, 1961. The four girls of Garabandal found out later that day and cried. They prayed for him both in their normal state and also when in ecstasy during the heavenly Lady's visits to them, until Saturday. They stopped praying for Fr. Luis on Saturday, August 12th, because the Virgin told them that Fr. Luis was now in Heaven. It seems that even this holy priest may have had to spend some time in Purgatory.

At 4:00 AM on August 16th, the Virgin told the girls that Fr. Luis would speak to them the next day. And so it happened, between 8:00 and 9:00 the following morning. They did not see him but only heard him. His voice sounded exactly as it had sounded while he was on earth. For a certain period of time Fr. Luis spoke to the young girls on twelve different occasions. These conversations between Heaven and earth are described in other books on the events that took place in Garabandal.

In the evening of August 17, 1961, the Blessed Virgin told the four girls that they would hear a strange voice calling them but not to be afraid. Suddenly they were enveloped in darkness and heard a mysterious, distant voice that frightened them—especially Mari Cruz. When the Virgin Mary reappeared to them, their fright disappeared. No explanation was given to them of whose voice they heard or why. This event still remains a mystery, at least for now.

Non-Fiction

On September 15, 1961, Feast of Our Lady of Sorrows, the Virgin showed the girls what is called the "Film of sinners." The girls were terrified and exclaimed: *"No, no! . . . What horror! How hideous! Take that away (from our sight). . . Yes, sacrifices (for sinners)! ...* And they begged pathetically for Divine Mercy on sinners.

On October 1, 1961, Our Lady of Mount Carmel de Garabandal told something very important to Conchita. It had to do with a future "major Church event" in which there would be the "reunification of the Christians."

And now we come to October 18, 1961, the day that the Virgin, on July 4th, had told the girls to make known the message that had appeared beneath Archangel Michael during his visits in June and early July.

October 18th was a miserable day in many ways—cold, rainy, muddy, hail, and even snow.

The revealing of the message was to be at 10:30 PM according to the instructions from the heavenly Lady. No predictions of any type of miracle had been made, but many of the people who came to Garabandal that day were looking for a miracle or at least something exciting. The message was to be made known at the church door, but church officials from the diocesan chancery in Santander didn't want any sign of prior ecclesiastical approval to be associated with whatever might be in the message, and they thought the message should be read to the people at 8:30 or 9:00 PM.

The waiting in the rain was becoming more and more intolerable to the people. At 8:00 PM, the pastor, Fr. Marichalar, sensing the pressure of the church officials from Santander and the mood of the people, sought out the girls to get them to move ahead with the public disclosure of the message. Soon the rumor spread rapidly: *"To the pines! To the pines!"*

The attempted dash of the people up to the pines at the top of the bluff turned out to be a nightmare in the heavy rain and mud. People fell down, slid backwards and had all manner of difficulties ascending the steep terrain. Fr. Marichalar was feeling quite uncomfortable, for Conchita had already told him the content of the message. He thought, then, that it was somewhat childish and that the people were not going to like it, especially since so many were expecting something spectacular. He kept to the rear of the crowd.

Finally about 10:00 PM, the girls handed him the message to read as they had been instructed. It was handwritten on a little piece of paper and signed by all four girls. Fr. Marichalar read it privately and handed it back to the girls for them to read aloud. In their youthful style they read the message aloud but not loud enough for everyone. So, two men read it again in a louder voice.

The First Formal Message:

"We must make many sacrifices, perform much penance, and visit the Blessed Sacrament frequently. But first we must be very good. If we do not, a Chastisement will befall us. The cup is already filling up, and if we do not change, a very great chastisement will come upon us." (October 18, 1961)

The physical and social environments of the night of October 18, 1961, at Garabandal, considering the bad weather, the mood of the people, and the digressions from the Virgin's instructions, was not conducive to high spirits at all. The people were quite disappointed, especially those who had expected a miracle or something extraordinary, or those who expected a message more appealing to their pre-conceived notions. The girls never predicted a miracle or anything spectacular, nor did they hint at any aspects of the message before the day of its revelation.

When time passed and serious thought was given to the apparently overly simple message, wiser reflection brought the realization that the message had profound meaning appropriate to the times, especially to the ensuing years.

However, the Great Lady's message was poorly heeded and not made known in the Church or the world to any sufficient degree. Only a very tiny fraction of humanity is aware of that message, and of those who are aware, one might wonder how many live that message.

The apparitions continued, and almost four years later, on the night of June 18, 1965, a second, formal message was given to one of the girls, Conchita, who had been told about it by the Virgin on January 1, 1965. The Virgin requested the Archangel Michael to deliver it to Conchita on June 18th. She later told Conchita that She had been too sorrowful to deliver it Herself.

The Second Formal Message:

> **As my message of October 18th (1961) has not been complied with and has not been made known to the world, I am advising you that this is the last one. Before, the cup was filling up. Now it is flowing over. Many cardinals, many bishops and many priests are on the road to perdition and are taking many souls with them. Less and less importance is being given to the Eucharist. You should turn the wrath of God away from yourselves by your efforts. If you ask for His forgiveness with sincere hearts, He will pardon you. I, your mother, through the intercession of Saint Michael the Archangel, ask you to amend your lives. You are now**

receiving the last warnings. I love you very much and do not want your condemnation. Pray to us with sincerity and we will grant your requests. You should make more sacrifices. Think about the passion of Jesus. (June 18, 1965)

In spite of the serious pleas of the Heavenly Mother, whom Jesus had given to humanity as He was dying on the cross, these formal and serious messages for all mankind, as well as the great drama of events that took place in San Sebastian de Garabandal, have been largely ignored, and basically "swept under the rug" by parties within the Catholic Church to whom these messages and events were directed, primarily for the benefit of the entire world. It isn't out of bounds to suspect that many of those who were mentioned specifically in the message of June 18, 1965— Cardinals, Bishops, and Priests—have been prone to ignoring or denying their reality. But this is not to say that a good number of humble priests and members of the Church Hierarchy have ignored or resisted these things; rather, they have listened, unlike the others.

Note to Non-Catholic Readers:

The Catholic Church honors Mary, the Mother of Jesus, with many titles, because Jesus, who is God, created his own mother with the qualities and the highest dignity to be so intimate with Him not only in her maternal role but also as His close collaborator in the great Mystery of Redemption. She not only always did His Will, but She never did her own will in anything. In addition to the love Jesus has for everyone in general, He also has a unique and special love for Her.

In these modern times, God has wanted Mary to become better known and loved, especially in her role as the true spiritual mother of all mankind.

It might be confusing at times to read about Her under one title and then under another. But no matter the title used for Her, it is always the same person, Mary.

Chapter Three

Prophets and Prophecy in the Christian Era

(An instruction for the remainder of this book)

As revealed in the Old Testament of the Bible, the Creator of the human race tolerated with invincible patience the ruination of his beautiful plan for mankind, when Adam freely chose to do his own will and disobey the little command to refrain from touching the Tree of the Knowledge of Good and Evil or to eat its fruit. Adam's disobedience and withdrawal from his pristine relationship with his God, his Father, the Author of his life was a very great wound to the Loving Heart of God and to the human race that would come forth from Adam and his spouse, Eve.

In His foreknowledge of all things, the Supreme Being, knew that Adam would fail his little test of obedience and the very sad results that would follow. Still, the Supreme Being would not fail in bringing about his ideal for mankind—the very purpose for which man was created. But both He and mankind would have to wait. The effects of Adam's disobedience would bring a delay accompanied by much suffering and disorder for the human race. The human race, so weakened by Adam's failure to maintain his original relationship with his God, would need a lot of assistance from its Creator in its long and dangerous trek back to the ideal relationship intended by God for his beloved human beings. This restoration of man's original relationship with the Supreme Being is infallibly bound to the glorious day of the fulfillment of the Prayer of His Only Begotten Son, known as the "Lord's Prayer" or the "Our Father."

The coming glorious and happy day of the restoration of man's original relationship with God will be the subject of the last chapters of this book. But first must come all the chapters that relate to present times and the terrible near future, and this requires an understanding of how the providence of the Supreme Being still mercifully uses prophecy in the Christian Era prior to exercising his Justice, which He resorts to when it becomes necessary to reset the course of his beloved but wayward children.

In the Old Testament of the Bible, God frequently communicated messages and prophecies to humanity, usually through men that He had chosen for the role of prophets, though He sometimes spoke his message directly to the person or persons for whom his message was intended. And there were times when God sent Angels from Heaven in the form of the appearance of men to give warnings to people on earth. Most of the men whom God called to be prophets of divine chastisements in the Old Testament times were despised and persecuted.

The Old Testament prophets have been categorized as major and minor prophets based on the length of their testimonies of God's revelation to them. Some of the major prophets are Daniel, Jeremiah, Isaiah and Ezekiel. There were many minor prophets, some of whom are Osee (Hoshea), Amos, Joel, Jonah, Micah, and Zechariah.

In the strict sense, prophecy refers in most cases to the foreknowledge of future things to happen. God alone knows the future. He knows it with certainty and in every respect. In his Mercy, He warns humanity in advance when punishment is necessary for correction. At other times He provides the knowledge of future events for our spiritual nourishment and hopeful anticipation, or to give proofs (when fulfilled) as advance signs of the authenticity of more serious prophecies. The role of the prophet is to make known to others what is represented to the mind of the prophet, according to the supernatural mode, in words or signs used by God to enlighten the prophet's mind of future things.

Although the gift of prophecy requires a special grace from God, He does not confine this grace to any particular class of persons or require any special preparation of the prophet in advance of receiving this gift. The special grace of prophecy is not a permanent grace but a grace given at the required time for its use.

God has given the grace of prophecy to angels, to men, women, and children, to Jews and gentiles, to popes, saints, mystics, and even to heathens and devils—all according to the purpose of His wisdom. Concerning the secrets of one's heart, no one else has access to them except God alone, who sometimes reveals these secrets to another for his divine purposes, as He did to Daniel concerning King Nebuchadnezzar's dream.

When the Eternal Decree of Redemption was to be fulfilled in the realm of time, God sent an Angel to announce to the prophesied Virgin that She had been elected to be the Mother of the Redeemer and that her "fiat" or "yes" was necessary for the Word to assume human nature. She was startled at the appearance of the Angel and his announcement and wondered how this request of God would be fulfilled, for She had consecrated her holy life to the state of virginity. When the Angel explained, She gave her "yes" and instantly became the Mother of God. The Word who is God, Second Person of Eternal Trinity, became incarnate in her chaste womb. The divine and Most Holy Redeemer had carefully prepared this elect Virgin whom He had specially created to be his mother. He had worked a miracle of Grace in

Her who was to have so intimate a relationship with Him, for nothing unholy or in the least defiled by sin would be proper to the one who would bear and nurture the Holy One. Later, after He had completed the Redemption of man and established the Church that would teach his redemptive and sanctifying doctrine and administer his sanctifying Grace, this holy Virgin, his own Mother would sit at his right hand with the role of Queen of Heaven and Earth and spiritual mother of humanity. And at the proper time the Most High would ask this Heavenly Queen to exercise a special, prophetical role on behalf of his beloved children on earth.

During his life on earth, the Son of God, Jesus, made prophecies of future events as did his apostles following his Ascension to Heaven from the Mount of Olives, forty days after his Resurrection on the first Easter Sunday. Then at various times and places, prophecies continued throughout Christian history. The source of these prophecies has been the Mercy of God whose purpose is to warn his children when they are straying off course from the way to eternal happiness in Heaven. To accomplish this purpose of Mercy, He has given the authentic grace of prophecy to men, women, and children—usually to certain holy women, and in recent times, mostly to children (examples: La Salette, Lourdes, Fatima, Garabandal, and others). But He has also given this special gift to some of the popes.

Suddenly and Unexpectedly

Over the past 42 years, following an unique experience in 1970 in New York City, the author has become keenly aware of God's all-out attempt to move the hearts of men to cease their perilous march to perdition by having the Queen of Heaven make visits to innocent children in various and remote places to give them prophetic messages for all of mankind. There have been very many of these events and many books and other literature written about them, but the merciful pleadings from Heaven have been ignored by most of humanity. We have now arrived at the critical moments, for not only will our possessions be taken away, but our very beings will experience the most terrible things imaginable. Survivors will see and feel things that have never happened before, some of which will be very, very good, especially that which is made known in chapters ten and eleven.

With this said, may what is contained in the following chapters be understood and accepted for the Glory of God and the salvation and sanctification of souls.

Pray and read and you will know the most important things that are coming.

Chapter Four

The Awful

The awesome things that had been happening in San Sebastian de Garabandal continued at a somewhat lesser pace through the winter and into the Spring of 1962. In addition to what has already been described above, the almost daily phenomena including the girls' ability to always recognize who were priests among the people, even when they were dressed in civilian clothes; the reading of hearts and knowledge of the thoughts of others (an infallible sign of the divine origin of the source of the phenomena taking place in Garabandal), the rapid, ecstatic flights by foot (forward or backward) of the girls when following the Virgin both in the day and in the night, dialogues between the girls and the Lady from Heaven which were recorded on tape, and numerous other acts, quite beyond the normal, which drew the pious amazement of the people and had a powerful, beneficial effect on the souls of many.

Suddenly and Unexpectedly

Then on June 19 and June 20, 1962, came the *two nights of the screams* reported in Chapter One.

The following is an account of what caused the screams. Separating what the girls saw on the first and second nights is not that simple, because most of what they revealed did not come out until several years later, and it seems that some of the girls' reports were worded in such a way that their memories may have blended the two separate nights' experiences to some degree.

The First Night of the Screams lasted 50 minutes and the young girls were shown primarily visions of the future *"Sudden and Unexpected Tribulation of Communism, led by Russia,"* during which Russia will gain dominion of the whole world. *"Russia will rule the world."*

It was 10:30 PM on June 19, 1962, when the people heard Mari Loli and Jacinta begin to scream horribly, causing great fright and concern to the people who were remaining obediently at the designated spot in the "calleja."

The two girls were shown the terrible persecution of Communism which would overrun Europe, where the rivers would turn red with blood. The Communist Tribulation would go beyond Europe to gain dominion of the whole world. The Catholic Church will seem to disappear, its buildings would be destroyed or locked, the Priests will have to go into hiding, and it seems that many would be martyred. The Sacraments would be very difficult to receive, if at all. This great tribulation would be very intense but not of a long duration, because when all hope seems lost, God Himself will bring it all to a stop with what is called the WARNING* to all mankind, revealing to each individual on earth the state of his or her soul as it exists before God. (*see Chapter Five)

> "Their tear-stained faces and incoherent speech immediately afterwards attested to the trauma experienced by Jacinta, Mari Loli and Mari Cruz during the first night of screams and it doesn't appear that they gave many details of what they experienced for quite some time."
>
> [*Garabandal Journal.* Editor: Barry Hanratty]

Mari Loli seems to have been the first to speak about it when, in 1967, she provided information to a Mexican priest, who was promoting the awareness of these events. Three years later, the same information, in the possession of Maria Saraco, had been written down and confirmed by Mari Loli with her own signature. It reads as follows:

> "In spite of continuing to see the Virgin, [during the first night of screams] we saw a great multitude of people who were suffering intensely and screaming in terror. The Blessed Virgin explained to us that this Great Tribulation, which was not even the Chastisement*,

would come because a time would arrive when the Church would appear to be on the point of perishing. It would pass through a terrible trial. We asked the Virgin what this great trial was called, and she told us it was 'Communism.'" (*She Went in Haste to the Moutain* by Eusebio Garcia de Pesquera, O.F.M. Cap.)

*The Chastisement refers to the terrible punishment of the world that God Himself will send if we do not repent and stay repentant after the Warning which ends the Communist Tribulation, corrects the conscience of the world, and is followed by the Great Miracle.]

This first revelation about the sudden and unexpected Communist Tribulation would be expanded upon further by the visionaries in later years, mostly through interviews with some of the girls as they grew older.

"The first of these trials has been named the Tribulation and will amount to an all-out attempt by Russia and its allies to turn the world into a confederacy of communist states. There will be bloodshed and great turmoil, and a persecution of the Church that will be, in the words of Blessed Pius IX, 'beyond description.' (Prophecy is one of the charisms of the papacy.)" —B. Hanratty, editor of *Garabandal Journal.* [Note: Pope Pius IX died in 1878.]

Mari Loli Mazon and Jacinta Gonzalez in June 1962, were shown the future *Great Chastisement* that will come directly from God and the much more imminent *Great Tribulation of Communism* which will come from man. A "sudden and unexpected" Tribulation of

43

Communism led by Russia will have an effect on the whole world, and will happen before the *Divine Warning* to the entire human race. *This Great Tribulation of Communism* is not the future *Chastisement of Fire.* That will come directly from God if man does not become and remain changed for the better following the Communist Tribulation, and also the Divine Warning, and Great Miracle to be described in Chapter Five and Chapter Six.

Readers may be wondering about the Islamic Jihad so much in the news in our day. The Virgin at Garabandal apparently never spoke about Islam or the radical followers of Islam, but She certainly did speak several times about Communism that "will come back."

Because the approaching events revealed by the Queen of Heaven, who is the Mother of Jesus, to the young girls of San Sebastian de Garabandal are of almost unsurpassable human importance, additional emphasis will be given by more descriptions, even if redundant.

> In 1967 Mari Loli said, "...The Blessed Virgin explained to us that this great Tribulation, which was not even the Chastisement, would come because a time would arrive when the Church would appear to be on the point of perishing. It would pass through a terrible trial. We asked the Virgin what this great trial was called and she told us it was Communism.
>
> (*She Went in Haste to the Mountain* by Eusebio Garcia de Pesquera, O.F.M. Cap.)

Suddenly and Unexpectedly

On November 14, 1965, German journalist Albrecht Weber interviewed Conchita and eventually wrote a book on Garabandal which was received by Pope John Paul II. The pope sent Mr. Weber a message through his secretary, Msgr. Dwivicz, encouraging him to continue promoting Garabandal **before it is too late**. The pope also added a message in his own handwriting. Over the years Mr. Weber has had a number of conversations with Conchita. In one of his conversations with Conchita, recorded in his book, *"Garabandal — the Finger of God,"* he brought up the question: "When will the Warning* occur?"

> Conchita responded, "When communism comes again** everything will happen."
>
> Mr. Weber then asked, "What do you mean by comes again?"
>
> Conchita replied: "Yes, when it newly comes again."
>
> Weber: "Does that mean that communism will go away before that?"
>
> Conchita: "I don't know. The Blessed Virgin simply said 'when communism comes again'. " (Interview of November 14, 1965

---

*The Warning is discussed in Chapter Five.
**Following the1989-91 period, with the fall of the Berlin Wall and dissolution of the Soviet Union, it became widely believed that Russian-led communism had ended.

Non-Fiction

During the *First Night of Screams* the young girls of Garabandal were shown the coming **"sudden and unexpected"** great Tribulation of Communism, led by Russia, that would gain dominion over the whole world. During that time there would come great distress upon the world and rivers would run red with blood, the Church would seem to disappear, priests would have to go into hiding, the Sacraments would not be available. It would be so horrible that mankind would arrive at the point of losing all hope, and when the situation had reached its worst point, GOD HIMSELF will intervene... God will send the Warning to all mankind. The Great Miracle will follow within twelve months of the Warning, and there will be conversions of many nations, including Russia.

It seems that the greatest trauma and distress of this Tribulation will be felt in Europe. When Conchita visited the future Saint Padre Pio in 1966 at his monastery in San Giovanni Rotondo, Italy, he told her that the Great Miracle of Garabandal [to come] will be paid for by the blood of the Europeans—oceans of blood.

[Note: Some persons have thought that the Tribulation of Communism is simply a matter of political communism and socialism gaining hold throughout the world. That idea is not consistent with what the young girls have said or the fact of their bloodcurdling screams.]

Our Lady told Conchita that Communism will "come back" and that it will also come to Spain, but Spain would not suffer as intensely as the rest of Europe, apparently because it had suffered Communism in the 1930's. Conchita's Aunt Antonia testified that she heard the girls say, while in ecstasy, that "if we don't amend our ways, Russia will take possession of the whole world."

In an August 2006 interview with the well-informed German journalist, mentioned above, the author of this book and those with him were told that the Communists would go into the village of San Sebastian de Garabandal during the Tribulation for a few days and that some people in the village would be killed for their faith. The German journalist said he had been told by one of the girls of Garabandal that just prior to the "revolution" [his term for the Tribulation of Communism] he should go to Southern Spain or to Portugal.

How will he know when the "revolution" is imminent? It has to do with the Pope going to Moscow and his return to Rome. Issue #5 of the *"Garabandal Journal"* contains a statement from his book, *"Garabandal—The Finger of God,"* which says: "The pope will go to Russia, to Moscow. As soon as he returns to the Vatican, hostilities will break out in different parts of Europe."

"Few will see God": This most terrifying prediction of all is found in the statement signed by Mari Loli and Jacinta Gonzalez in June, 1962, at the time of the two "Nights of the Screams" in which the children were shown the future Great Tribulation of Communism (from man) and the later Great Chastisement (directly from God). In the girl's statement, they said that the Virgin told them that the world continues the same, that it has not changed at all and *"few will see God"*—so few that it is causing the Virgin great sorrow... These grave concerns of Our Lady in 1962 about the world not changing should be considered in the context of her formal message of October 18,1961. (Note: It goes without saying that the moral condition of humanity in 1962 was far, far less evil than today! The words, *"few will see God,"* are more terrifying than anything else already reported, because these words are equivalent to "only a few in these times will be saved from eternal damnation." According to other revelations in these times, which have the signs of being authentically coming from Heaven, human society has reached a degree of immorality far exceeding that of the days of Noah.

No one expects the coming Great Tribulation of Communism because the world has been lulled into the false belief that Communism has died with the fall of the Berlin Wall and the dissolution of the Soviet Union. In the United States of America, the entire leadership in Washington is oblivious to the fate awaiting the entire world, which is rapidly approaching. One possible exception (and there may be some others) is the Director of National Intelligence, James R. Clapper, who testified before a Senate hearing on March 10, 2011 that our greatest potential enemies are Russia and

China. However, he was laughed at by those who should have listened and learned.

In reality, though, it is ourselves who are our greatest enemies. Our own sins of apostasy, secularism, impurity, artificial birth control, abortion and so many other sins against the divinely ordained nature given us by God have blinded us to the reality and terrible consequences of our own sins, which are now far worse than in the days of Noah and those of Sodom and Gomorrah.

Interview with Mari Loli
October 19, 1982

Originally published in a 1990 Special Edition of "Garabandal" magazine by *The Workers of Our Lady of Mt. Carmel*

Q. Do you remember what the Blessed Mother said about the communist tribulation that is to precede the Warning?

A. It would look like the communists have taken over the whole world, and it would be very hard to practice the religion, for priests to offer Mass, or for the people to open the doors of the churches.

Q. Is that what you meant when you said that it would seem as though the Church had disappeared?

A. Yes.

Q. It would be because of the persecution and not because the people would stop practicing their religion?

A. Yes, but I guess a lot of people will stop. Whoever practices it will have to go into hiding.

Q. Will this only be in Europe or do you think it will be here in the United States as well?

A. I don't know because for me at that time, Europe was the whole world. I just assumed it was that way. The Blessed Mother didn't specify in what place. To me it looked like it was everywhere.

Q. Approximately 67% of the earth's land is now dominated by communism. Do you think that's sufficient to fulfill Our Lady's prophecy?

A. I really don't know. It sounded to me like it would be more than that.

Q. In other words you think it will be worse that it is now?

A. That's what I thought from what she said, but I really don't know exactly. To me it looked more like it was every place out there, the places I saw in my mind. In a lot of countries in Europe you can still practice your religion.

Q. So, the situation in the world is not bad enough for the Warning to happen?

A. The Warning is not going to happen yet, so it's probably going to get worse.

Suddenly and Unexpectedly

Q. You said that it would be very difficult for priests to offer Mass. Was this something that the Blessed Mother told you or was it something that you thought yourself because of the communist tribulation?

A. From what I remember, it was something She said.

Q. And the Virgin said that it would seem as though the Church had disappeared?

A. Yes.

Q. Did the Blessed Mother ever say anything about the Holy Father having to leave Rome at the time of the Warning?

A. No, But what it looked like to me—maybe at this time I was confusing in my mind what I was seeing and what the Blessed Mother was saying to me because it's been so many years—but what it looked like to me was that the pope couldn't be in Rome either, you know what I mean, out in the open. He was being persecuted, too, and had to hide just like everybody else.

Extract from Interview with Mari Loli
by Father Francis Benac, S. J.
September 29, 1978

Father Benac: Did the Blessed Virgin speak of Communism?

Mari Loli: Our Lady spoke several times about Communism. I don't remember how many times, but she said that a time would come when it would seem

51

that Communism had mastered or engulfed the whole world. I think it was then that she told us that Priests would have difficulty saying Mass, and talking about God and divine things.

Father Benac: Did Our Lady ever speak of people being put to death?

Mari Loli: What Our Lady said was that priests would have to go into hiding but I didn't see whether they were being killed or not. She didn't exactly say they would be killed, but I'm sure they would be martyred.

Father Benac: Your mother told me that one night you were upstairs with your father and that you cried and cried for one hour. Afterwards your father said to her: "I have just seen the most touching sight. Loli was crying the whole time while saying, 'Oh, it's going to be like that? People are going to suffer like that? Oh, make me suffer*!' " Do you remember what you said at the time?

Mari Loli: It was all related to communism and what is going to happen in the Church and to the people because all these things are to have repercussions amongst the people. When the Church suffers confusion, the people are going to suffer too. Some priests who are communists will create such confusion that people will not know right from wrong.

* Mari Loli wanted to suffer as her offering to help offset Divine Justice against sinners.

Interviews with Jacinta Gonzalez

August, 1979

Q. Do you recall anything about a great tribulation, communism...?

A. Yes, it was an invasion—well, something that was a great evil in which communism played a great part—but I no longer remember which countries or what region was stricken. The Blessed Virgin insisted in telling us to pray (that it be averted). These difficult events will take place before the Warning because the Warning itself will take place when the situation will be at its worst.

[Ref: Garabandal Interational Magazine October-December 2004]

April 16, 1983

Q. In the 1979 interview (above), you said in describing the communist tribulation that "it was like an invasion." Did you see scenes of this invasion?

A. Sometimes I confuse an invasion with a persecution.

(Ref: Garabandal Interational Magazine October-December 2004)

53

Chapter Five

The Warning

The Warning is a supernatural intervention on the part of God which will have as its divine and merciful purpose to correct the conscience of the world and bring an end to the Tribulation of Communism that will have engulfed the world. It will also serve as a profound humiliation of the pride of mankind in preparation for the Great Miracle which will follow the Warning within 12 months' time. During the Warning, everyone on earth will have an encounter with God, a type of mini-judgment, in which we will see the evil we have done, the good that we should have done—in sum, how God sees us as we really are. It will be of short duration but will seem longer due to its intensity. Each person will experience the Warning in an individual way, unaware of anything else.

Suddenly and Unexpectedly

Notice to Readers of this Book:

Most of the interviews with the girls of Garabandal were given several to many years after their experiences. They were not always able to remember clearly everything that they were asked about in the interviews. In addition, because of the seriousness of what was made known to them, they often use the word, "soon," when asked to give the times when the predicted events would occur. In some cases they were forbidden to give dates until the predicted event or events were about to occur. One example is that Conchita, although she gave the exact date of the coming Great Miracle to Pope Paul VI, she was instructed not to make the date public until 8 days prior to the date of the Great Miracle.

Interviews with Mari Loli Mazon

Originally published in a 1990 Special Edition of "Garabandal" magazine by *The Workers of Our Lady of Mt. Carmel*

July 27, 1975

Q. You have said that you know the year of the Warning. Can you tell us if it will occur in the next few years or is it still in the distant future?

A. No. I can't say anything.

Q. Did the Blessed Mother tell you not to speak about the Warning?

A. No, she didn't, but, because the Warning and the Miracle are within the same year,* I feel it inside not to say anything. [*It is more likely that she meant "within 12 months," based on other reports.]

55

Q. How do you know the Warning and the Miracle are within the same year? [Usually understood: To be within 12 months]

A. During an apparition—I don't remember just when—the Blessed Virgin told me.

Q. Reportedly, you have said that when the Warning occurs everything will stand still, even planes in the sky. Is this true?

A. Yes, but just for a few moments.

Q. You mean that everything will stop at a given moment and at that moment the Warning will occur?

A. Yes.

Q. When was this information revealed to you?

A. During an apparition the Blessed Virgin told me all this.

Q. Was all the information given you during one apparition, or did Our Lady tell you this over several apparitions?

A. She told me all of this during one apparition. I don't remember now if she spoke about the Warning during any other apparition.

Q. Do you know how long the Warning will last?

A. Just a few minutes.

Q. Are you afraid of the Warning?

A. Yes. Like everyone else, I have faults, and the Warning will show me my faults and this makes me afraid.

Q. Can you tell us anything else about the Warning?

A. All I can say is that it is very close* and that it is very important that we prepare ourselves because it will be a terrible thing. It will make us feel all the wrong we have done. [*Considering the magnitude of this event and lack of any precedence in human history it is understandable that she says "close."]

February, 1977

Q. Have you ever discussed with Conchita the dates of the Warning of which you know the year, and the Miracle which she knows?

A. I have never talked to Conchita about these dates.

Q. Have you any words of advice for the people in order that they might prepare for this event?

A. To do much penance, make sacrifices, visit the Blessed Sacrament every day that we are able to, and to pray the holy rosary daily.

September 29, 1978

Q. Since you are the one who knows the most about the Warning will you tell us if this event is to take place before the Miracle promised through Conchita Gonzalez?

A. Everyone will experience it wherever they may be, regardless of their condition or their knowledge of God...It will be an interior personal experience. it will look as if the world has come to a standstill,...however, no one will be aware of that as they will be totally absorbed in their own experience.

Q. About the nature of the Warning, how do you sense it:

A. It is going to be something like an interior feeling of sorrow and pain for having offended God. God will help us to see clearly the harm we are causing Him and all the evil things we do. He will help us to sense this interior pain because often when we do something wrong we just ask the Lord's forgiveness with our lips, but now (through the Warning) He will help us sense physically that deep sorrow.

Q. You said that when the Warning comes, the planes would stop in the air and that all engines would stop. Is this what the Blessed Mother told you?

A. She said that everything, everywhere, for a moment would stop and the people would just think and look inside themselves.

Q. Will there be any noise with the Warning like a wind blowing?

A. The way I saw it at the time, it was more like a big silence, like a sense of emptiness. Everything was very silent. That's the way I saw it.

Q. Seven years ago you said that the Warning was soon. Many people thought it would have happened by now. What would you say today?

A. It is soon. Everything looks soon to me because time goes by so fast.

Q. You're the only one who knows the year of the Warning. Did you ever tell it to anyone else, like a priest for example?

A. No.

Q. Will people be fighting with one another when the Warning comes?

A. (no answer)

Conchita Gonzalez

From a letter of June 2, 1965 referring to what she was told on January 1, 1965

"The Blessed Virgin told me (during a two-hour apparition at the pines January 1, 1965) that the warning would be given to the entire world before the miracle in order that the world might amend itself. It will come directly from God and be visible throughout the entire world. No one can escape it. We will feel it bodily and interiorly.

"The warning is like a chastisement, a terrifying thing for the good as well as for the wicked. It will be like a revelation of our sins. We shall see the consequences of the sins we have committed. God will send the warning to purify us so that we may better appreciate the miracle by which He clearly proves His love for us and hence His desire that we fulfill the message. The warning will draw the good closer to God and it will warn the wicked that the end of time is coming. It will be like fire. It will not burn our flesh but we will feel it bodily and interiorly."

Conchita Gonzalez

January 2, 1965

"This warning, like the chastisement, is a very fearful thing for the good as well as the wicked. It will draw the good closer to God and it will warn the wicked that the end of time* is coming and that these are the last warnings. No one can stop it from happening. It is certain, although I know nothing of the day or the date.

[*This is not to be confused with end of the world; and most other reports speak of this as "end of the times," which is generally understood to mean the definitive and permanent end of our present times. However, the meaning may have a special, eschatological meaning, not currently understood with clarity.]

"The warning will be like a revelation of our sins, and it will be seen and experienced equally by believers and non-believers and people of any religion whatsoever. Each person on earth will have an interior experience of how they stand in the light of God's Justice. It is like a purification for the miracle. And it is like a catastrophe. It will make us think of the dead, that is, we would prefer to be dead than to experience the warning. The warning will be recognized and accepted by the world.

"Jesus will send the warning to purify us so that we may better appreciate the miracle by which he clearly proves his love for us and hence his desire that we see the consequences of the sins we have committed. I think that those who do not despair will experience great good from it for their sanctification.

"The Warning is something supernatural and will not be explained by science. It will be seen and experienced by all men all over the world and will be a direct work of God. It will be very awesome. However, if men die from it, it will be only from the emotional shock of experiencing it. It will be a correction of the conscience of the world. Those who do not know Christ (non-Christians) will believe it is a warning from God."

In a letter dated June 2, 1965, Conchita writes: "The Blessed Virgin told me on the first of January that a Warning would be given before the Miracle so that the world might amend itself. This **Warning**, like the **Chastisement** (another prophesied event, worse that the Flood of Noah's time, to be explained in Chapter Seven), is a very fearful thing for the good as well as for the wicked. It will draw the good closer to God and it will warn the wicked that the end of time [time? or the times?] is coming and that these are the last warnings. There is more to it than this, but it can't be said by letter. No one can stop it from happening. It is certain, although I know nothing concerning the day or the date."

In another apparition, the year of the Warning was made known to Mari Loli, but she has felt strongly that she should not reveal the year.

Jacinta Gonzalez

January 2, 1965

"The Warning is something that is first seen in the air everywhere in the world and immediately is transmitted

61

into the interior of our souls. It will last for a very little time, but it will seem a very long time because of its effect within us. It will be for the good of our souls in order to see in ourselves our conscience; the good that we have failed to do, and the bad that we have done. Then we will feel a great love towards our Heavenly Parents and ask forgiveness for all our offenses. The Warning is for us to draw closer to Him and to increase our faith. Therefore, one should prepare for that day, but not await it with fear. God does not send things for the sake of fear but rather with justice and love. He does it for the good of all His children so they might enjoy eternal happiness and not be lost."

Mari Loli Mazon

January 2, 1965

"We will see it [the Warning] and feel it within ourselves, and it will be most clear that it comes from God."

"The Virgin Mary told Conchita, 'We should bear this suffering [experienced during the Warning] for the sake of her Son, victim of the gravest offenses.'"

"The Virgin Mary said that the Warning Marks the 'End of the Times.'"

[It seems that the expression "End of the Times" is like a line of historical demarcation, beyond which things will be entirely different and human behavior will change dramatically.]

According to later statements given by Jacinta, and published in the July-Sept. 1977 issue of the magazine

Suddenly and Unexpectedly

Needles, later titled *Garabandal:* "The Warning is something that is first seen in the air everywhere in the world and immediately is transmitted into the interior of our souls. It will last for a very little time, but it will seem a very long time because of its effect within us. It will be for the good of our souls—in order to see in ourselves our conscience. . . the good and the bad that we have done. . ."

It will come upon us like a fire from heaven, which we will feel profoundly in our interior. By its light each one will see the state of his soul with complete clearness; he will experience what it is to lose God; he will feel the purifying action of the cleansing flame. Briefly, it will be like having the Particular Judgment in one's very soul while still alive.

The purification of the Warning will be necessary to make us ready to face the Miracle. Otherwise we might not be able to sustain the superhuman and marvelous experience of the Miracle. Perhaps because he had not previously undergone the Warning, the early death of Fr. Luis Andreu came about, after he saw on that summer night in 1961 what even the visionaries have not yet seen.

— "I think, too, that the church would be the best place to pass it, there next to the Blessed Sacrament, so that He could support us, give us strength, and aid us to suffer it better."

———————

Article on the Warning

"Garabandal Journal"

(March-April 2012) by Barry Hanratty:

The Warning begins, according to Conchita, as a sighting in the sky but not a comet, meteor or anything of a physical nature, since it will be supernatural and "will not be explained by science." From the sky this *presence* descends into every soul to do its terrible [but beneficial] work. Conchita tells us: "Everyone in the whole world will see a sign, a grace, or a punishment within themselves. They will find themselves all alone in the world, no matter where they are at that time, alone with their conscience right before God."

Mari Loli said, "It will look as if the world had come to a standstill, however, no one will be aware of that as they will be totally absorbed in their own experience." Then, in this moment frozen in time, will come the reckoning. Conchita continues, "They will see all their sins and what their sins have caused." She also said that in addition to seeing the evil of our sins, we will also see all the good we have failed to do. She goes on, "It will not burn our bodies but we will feel it both physically and interiorly." And Mari Loli said, "It is going to be something like an interior feeling of sorrow and pain for having offended God. God will help us to see clearly the harm [offense] we are causing Him and all the evil things that we do. God will help us to sense that interior pain because often when we do something wrong we just ask with our lips for the Lord to forgive us, but now He will help us sense that deep sorrow."

Suddenly and Unexpectedly

Everyone on earth, including newborn babies (those still in the womb?) and the most advanced in age will experience it. But this experience will be personal for each individual depending on the state of their own soul.

Conchita put it this way to Dr. J. Dominguez, "We will all feel the *Aviso* [Spanish term for what we call the *Warning* in English] differently because it will be very personal. Therefore, we will all act differently to it because your sins are different from mine." While this does not necessarily mean that the better we are the less we will have to suffer, it stands to reason that it will be less traumatic for those in the state of grace than for hardened sinners. Conchita did say that Catholics will endure it better than others (does that include fallen-away Catholics?).

But when Conchita says that we will "all see a sign, a grace *or* a punishment" this seems to indicate that some will be exempt from suffering in whole or in part such as babies, the mentally retarded, the chronically ill and dying, and souls who have reached the highest stages of the interior life. But aside from these exceptions, no one else will be excluded. Souls who are further along in the spiritual life may have to suffer acutely for lesser infractions—St. Catherine of Genoa said that God finds fault with everything—so that He can draw them up higher. As Conchita said, "[The Aviso] will be for the good to draw closer to God and **for the others to amend their lives.**" —Barry Hanratty

Barry Hanratty is the editor of *Garabandal Journal* and one of the world's top experts on the history of Garabandal.

Non-Fiction

Chapter Six

THE GREAT MIRACLE

"The Miracle *will take place within one year after the Warning."* Conchita will announce the miracle eight days prior to its occurrence. The Miracle will take place at the pine grove and will be visible to all who are in the village or the surrounding mountains, In Conchita's words the miracle will be "very great because the world's needs are very great." It will be "a miracle of the love of God, something that will manifest His love in an astounding way."

It will be God's greatest ever public Miracle. The Miracle of the Sun at Fatima in 1917, momentous and unprecedented as it was, will seem insignificant in comparison.

Suddenly and Unexpectedly

Conchita: *"The Blessed Virgin advised me of a great Miracle, saying that God, Our Lord, would perform it through her intercession. Just as the chastisement will be very, very great, in keeping with the needs of the world.*

"The Blessed Virgin has told me the date of the miracle and what it will consist of. I am supposed to announce it eight days in advance, so that people will come. The Pope will see it from wherever he is, and Padre Pio also. [He did see the miracle before he died]. The sick who are present at the miracle will be cured and the sinners will be converted.

"It will coincide with a happy event in the Church and with the feast of a saint who is a martyr of the Eucharist, and it will take place at eight-thirty on a Thursday evening. It will be visible not only to all those who are in the village but also to those in the surrounding mountains. It will be the greatest miracle that Jesus has performed for the world. There won't be the slightest doubt that it comes from God and that it is for the good of mankind. A permanent sign will remain forever as a result of the great miracle. It will be of supernatural origin and something that has never been seen before on earth.

"There will be no doubt in the mind of anyone who sees this great miracle which God, Our Lord, will perform

through the intercession of the Blessed Virgin. And now as we await this great day of the miracle, let us see if the world changes and the chastisement is averted."

On September 14, 1965, Conchita said: "The sign that will remain forever at the pines is something we will be able to photograph, televise and see, but not touch. It will be evident that it is not a thing of this world but from God." At another time, concerning the great Miracle, she added that, "it would last about 15 minutes." On August 10, 1971, while talking to a group of Americans, she offered this revealing information: "It will take place on or between the eighth and sixteenth of March, April or May. It will not happen in February or June." Eight days in advance of the Miracle Conchita will give notice to the world about its coming.

In an interview that this author and other persons had around year 2002 with Christine Bocabeille, who was part of the original ad hoc team to investigate the events of Garabandal with Fr. Laffineur in the 1960s, we learned some remarkable things that are to take place during the coming Great Miracle. It is well known in the literature about Garabandal that Our Lady said regarding those who are present in Garabandal and the surrounding mountains at the time of the Miracle "the sick will be cured, the unbelievers will believe, and the sinners will convert." What is not generally known and what Christine Bocabeille told us in her interview was this:

Suddenly and Unexpectedly

"During the Great Miracle, we will see the Glory of God!" But we won't die,* because we will be given a special grace to prevent us from dying. Christine Bocabeille went on to say that we will sensibly feel the indwelling Trinity within us during the Miracle, and Priests will also sensibly experience the interior presence of Jesus affirming His presence within them when they pronounce the words of consecration during the Holy Sacrifice of the Mass. [*Scripture says that no one can see God and live.]

Let's not forget that two holy Priests have seen in advance the coming Great Miracle. One of these Priests is St. Padre Pio (1887-1968)—canonized in 2002, who vigorously affirmed the truth of what happened at San Sebastian de Garabandal (1961-1965). The other is Fr. Luis Andreu, S.J., who, as described in Chapter Two, died of joy shortly after seeing the Miracle on August 8, 1961.

Immediately following the Great Miracle, God will place a Sign from Heaven above the pine trees at the top of the bluff where the Great Miracle just occurred. This sign will be visible and photographable but cannot be felt by the sense of touch or moved. It will endure until the end of the world. It is anticipated that people from all parts of the world will be coming continuously to Garabandal to see this permanent sign from Heaven.

Chapter Seven

THE CHASTISEMENT
–FIRE FROM HEAVEN–

*For when they shall say, peace and security; then shall
sudden destruction come upon them, as the pains upon her
that is with child, and they shall not escape.* (Thes 5: 3)

*Behold, the day of the LORD comes, cruel, with wrath and
fierce anger, to make the earth a desolation and to destroy
its sinners from it.*

*For the stars of the heavens and their constellations will not
give their light; the sun will be dark at its rising and the
moon will not shed its light. I will punish the world for its evil,
and the wicked for their iniquity.* (Isaiah 13: 6-13)

The Two Formal Messages given to the world by Our
Lady of Mt. Carmel at Garabandal, warned of a terrible
Chastisement with which God would punish humanity if
people did not repent and change their ways.

Suddenly and Unexpectedly

The first of these Messages was made known to the young girls at Garabandal on July 4, 1961, but they were told to make it public on October 18, 1961, which they did.

The second Message was given on June 18, 1965 and was more forceful and Our Lady's pain of heart is obvious. She even asked St. Michael the Archangel to deliver the message in her stead.

Both Messages are found in Chapter Two, but here are the parts referring to the Chastisement of Fire from Heaven if we don't repent and change our ways.

The Message of October 18, 1961, includes these words: **"The cup is already filling up, and if we do not change, a very great chastisement will come upon us. . ."**

It is more than obvious that since 1961 human society, instead of changing for the better has changed exceedingly for the worse!

The Message of June 18, 1965, includes these words: **"As my message of October 18 [1961] has not been complied with and has not been made known to the world, I am advising you that this is the last one. Before, the cup was filling up. Now it is flowing over. Many cardinals, many bishops and many priests are on the road to perdition and are taking many souls with them. . ."**

Non-Fiction

These extracts from the two formal messages are about the Great Chastisement of Fire that comes after all three of the following events have been completed:

(1) The terrifying, bloody and unprecedented Tribulation of Communism that will come **"suddenly and unexpectedly."**

(2) The Warning from God to every person on earth, which ends the Tribulation of Communism and corrects the conscience of the world.

(3) The Great Miracle to take place at San Sebastian de Garabandal within the twelve-month period following the Warning.

Our Lady said that as a consequence of the Warning and Miracle, many nations, including Russia, would be converted. Therefore it is reasonable to speculate that immediately following the Great Miracle, there will be a time of conversion and evangelization throughout the world. However, it is probable that after a time, perhaps 25–30 years, humanity will regress toward its former, grievously sinful ways.

This Great Chastisement of Fire from Heaven will come if humanity does revert to its former, evil ways at some point after the Great Miracle. Three of the young girls of Garabandal were shown the Great Chastisement of Fire on the night of June 20, 1962, and they screamed for more than three hours as they watched!

Suddenly and Unexpectedly

From Chapter Two, here again is the entire message of the Queen of Prophets given through St. Michael the Archangel on June 18, 1965 :

As my message of October 18th has not been complied with and has not been made known to the world, I am advising you that this is the last one. **Before, the cup was filling up. Now it is flowing over.** *Many cardinals, many bishops and many priests are on the road to perdition and are taking many souls with them. Less and less importance is being given to the Eucharist. You should turn the wrath of God away from yourselves by your efforts. If you ask for His forgiveness with sincere hearts, He will pardon you. I, your mother, through the intercession of Saint Michael the Archangel, ask you to amend your lives. You are now receiving the last warnings. I love you very much and do not want your condemnation. Pray to us with sincerity and we will grant your requests. You should make more sacrifices. Think about the passion of Jesus. (June 18, 1965)*

The contents of the **"cup"** are the wrath of Divine Indignation and Justice due to an overwhelmingly offended God—a God of Infinitely Magnanimous Love.

Non-Fiction

The young girls of Garabandal were shown the Chastisement that would come directly from the hand of God upon the human race. Here is only a portion of what they saw:

In response to a question by Maria Herrero de Gallardo on October 7, 1962, about the nights of the screams on June 19 and 20, 1962, Mari Loli Mazon said:

> *"Oh!. That was horrible to see. We were really frightened, and I know no words that could explain it. We saw rivers change into blood*.... **Fire fell from the sky**** .... And something much worse still, which I'm not able to reveal now.****

> *"In spite of continuing to see the Virgin, (during the Nights of the Screams) we saw a great multitude of people who were suffering intensely and screaming in terror. The Blessed Virgin explained to us that this great tribulation, which was not even the Chastisement, would come because a time would arrive when the Church would appear to be on the point of perishing. It would pass through a terrible trial. We asked the Virgin what this great trial was called and she told us it was "Communism." Then she showed us how the great Chastisement for all mankind would come, and that it would come directly from God.*

Suddenly and Unexpectedly

"At a certain moment, not a single motor or machine would function; a terrible heat wave will strike the earth and men will begin to feel a great thirst. In desperation they will seek water, but this will evaporate from the heat. Then almost everyone will despair and they will seek to kill one another. But they will lose their strength and fall to the ground. Then it will be understood that it is God alone Who has permitted this.

"Then we saw a crowd in the midst of flames. The people ran to hurl themselves into the lakes and seas. But the water seemed to boil, and instead of putting out the flames, it seemed to enkindle them even more. It was so horrible that I asked the Blessed Virgin to take all the young children with her before all this happened. But the Virgin told us that by the time it came, they would all be adults."

(Note: As the time of producing this book in 2012, those "young children" that Mari Loli referred to would now be in their fifties.)

---

* This refers to the Great Tribulation of Communism
** This refers to the Chastisement of Fire from Heaven
***(?) A possible reference to souls falling into Hell by the hundreds of millions or even of billions, which would be consistent with the Virgin's June 1962 words to the girls of Garabandal, that in the context of our times "Few will see God." This possibility is also consistent with the vision of Hell that Mary showed the three shepherd children at Fatima on July 13, 1917. Let us pray that the merciful Warning and Miracle will change such a possible, everlasting disaster.

Non-Fiction

Another of the young girls, Conchita Gonzales once said:

> "I have seen the Chastisement. I can assure you that if it comes, it is worse than being enveloped in fire, worse than having fire above and beneath you. I do not know how much time will elapse between the Miracle and the Chastisement.
>
> "If we do not change, the Chastisement will be terrible, in keeping with what we deserve. We saw it, but I cannot say what it consists of because I do not have permission from the Blessed Virgin to do so... When I saw it, I felt a very great fear, and that notwithstanding I was looking at the Blessed Virgin at the same time."

On another occasion, as an adult, Conchita gave this statement:

> "We are now in the last warnings, in the final moments. God has already prepared us for all the last things, even the Chastisement, for it is needed. The Chastisement must come because the Miracle will not suffice by itself to make us change. It is true that we will change after seeing the Miracle, but then we will fall again. That is why all of us who hear these words should prepare ourselves and induce all those around us, all those within our reach, to change their lives . . .

Suddenly and Unexpectedly

"However, it will not be possible to avoid the Chastisement because we have now lost even the sense of sin. We have reached such an extremity that God cannot now avoid sending the Chastisement. We need it for our own good. **Those who survive the Chastisement will change very much, and then we shall live for God until the end of time, which will also arrive."**

Concerning Conchita's statement at that time about the impossibilty of avoiding the Chastisment, she admitted to Fr. Joseph Pelletier that this was her opinion. Our Lady had said it would happen if we don't change. Nevertheless, other equally valid sources known to the Church, independent of the Events of Garabandal, and made known prior to those events, speak of the Chastisement as certain.

On yet another occasion, Conchita wisely commented, "Terror and fear are not the best means to move souls." And Barry Hanratty, editor of "Garabandal Journal" has written: "To dwell too much on the destructive nature of the Chastisement could lead to moroseness and would oppose a healthy spiritual outlook. Everything happens within the providence of God even the Chastisement if it should come. If it does happen, it will be because that is the best and most necessary thing to happen at that particular time. And even in this cataclysmic event can be seen divine mercy. If the glory of God in the world is on the verge of being overwhelmed by evil, He will intervene to preserve the good."

Something of great significance should be pointed out in reference to Conchita's statement, **"Those who survive the Chastisement will change very much and then we will live for God until the end of time, which will also arrive."**

This insight given to Conchita can be understood as referring to the time of the universal Reign of the Divine Will on earth as in Heaven, which Christians have been praying for in the Lord's Prayer for 2,000 years: that the Father's Kingdom come so that His Will be done on earth the same way as in Heaven. It seems to this author that the end of time would come when the glory of God is completed by those who will live in the Kingdom of the Divine Will.

The marvelous subject of the Reign of the Divine Will will be given serious attention in Chapters Ten and Eleven of this book.

Chapter Eight

When Will These Things Happen?
–The Foretellings–

First, let us be reminded of the most important messages given at Garabandal and the still pending predictions:

1. The First Formal Message of October 18, 1961:

> "We must make many sacrifices, perform much penance, and visit the Blessed Sacrament frequently. But first we must be very good. If we do not, a Chastisement will befall us. The cup is already filling up, and if we do not change, a very great chastisement will come upon us."

2. The Two Nights of the Screams on June 19 and June 20, 1962:

On the first night of the screams the girls screamed for 50 minutes having been shown the future Tribulation of Communism that would come one day, suddenly and unexpectedly, and will gain dominion of the whole world.

On the second night of the screams the girls screamed for three hours having seen the future Chastisement of fire from Heaven. The Chastisement will come at some unknown time after a Great Miracle, mentioned below.

3. The Miracle of the Eucharistic Host on July 19, 1962:

This "small" miracle, predicted in advance, actually occurred in the early hours of July 19, 1962, although it had been predicted for July 18. The delay was due to either or both of the following reasons: The unruly, worldly atmosphere of some people in the village that night and the fact that Conchita had already taken Holy Communion at morning Mass on the eighteenth. In 1962, Church rules allowed the reception of Holy Communion only once per day.

Suddenly and Unexpectedly

The miracle of the Host consisted of one of the young girls, Conchita, receiving the Eucharistic Host visibly on her tongue from St. Michael the Archangel. She had already received the Eucharistic Host many times before, but invisibly. This miracle was photographed.

4. The Second Formal Message of June 18, 1965:

As my message of October 18th has not been complied with and has not been made known to the world, I am advising you that this is the last one. Before, the cup was filling up. Now it is flowing over. Many cardinals, many bishops and many priests are on the road to perdition and are taking many souls with them. Less and less importance is being given to the Eucharist. You should turn the wrath of God away from yourselves by your efforts. If you ask for His forgiveness with sincere hearts, He will pardon you. I, your mother, through the intercession of Saint Michael the Archangel, ask you to amend your lives. You are now receiving the last warnings. I love you very much and do not want your condemnation. Pray to us with sincerity and we will grant your requests. You should make more sacrifices. Think about the passion of Jesus.

[Note: This formal message was delivered by St. Michael the Archangel on behalf Our Lady because the message was too sorrowful for Her to deliver Herself because of what had to be said of her beloved Priests.]

5. Prediction of a Warning from God to every Person on Earth:

This supernatural intevention of God will stop the coming Communist Tribulation and change the Conscience of the World. It will happen in an even-numbered year and prior to the Great Miracle.

6. The coming Greatest Public Miracle in all History:

The Great Miracle will take place at Garabandal and occur within 12 months after the Warning in the spring of a future year between the 8th and 16th of a month in that future spring. It will take place on a Thursday evening at 8:30 PM. It will coincide with a happy event in the Church and will occur on the feast day of a Saint whose martyrdom was related to the Eucharist.

The Great Miracle will take place at Garabandal. The sick there will be cured, the sinners will be converted, the unbelievers will believe, and best of all, the people there will see the Glory of God and not die. The Miracle has already been seen in advance by two Catholic Priests— Fr. Luis Andeu, S.J., who died of joy shortly after seeing the Miracle on August 8, 1961 and St. Padre Pio, OFM Cap., who saw the Miracle shortly before his death in 1968.

7. There will be a Unification of the Churches:

After the miracle, Russia will be converted and also many other nations. It seems that Russia will become an example to other nations, including the USA. The Churches will unite.

8. Chastisement of Fire from Heaven:

If the people of the world drift back to godlessness at some point after the Miracle, God will send a Chastisement of Fire from Heaven. Other sources clearly predict a long period of true holiness and happiness following the Chastisement, which seems to be the "Day of the Lord" mentioned in Isaiah 13: 6-13.

Ascertaining the Times of the Great Predicted Events

Note: Making our own predictions of unknown dates of future events is imprudent, for God alone knows the future. And He alone has the absolute right to make known future dates to whom He pleases. In the Holy Bible, God has given certain signs for us to gain a general understanding of when major things will occur. But God also has the right to give us more urgent and clearer signs when such events are imminent. The evidence is overwhelming that God has sent Mary, the Mother of Jesus, to inform us of imminent, serious events, their sequence and their consequences. Due to the rapidly changing events in our time (as this book is being written in 2012) it seems proper to restate some details that give signs for each reader to discern for himself.

At San Sebastian de Garabandal (1961–1965) the Queen of Prophets came from Heaven to warn the human family on earth of the terrible and unprecedented events soon to come, which will mark the end of the present era and the beginning of a new and very happy era for those who survive. She also gave sufficient information about the timing of these predicted events, thus giving additonal credence to her attempts to help save as many souls as possible.

The *key prophetic prediction* is the Great Miracle to come, because it is the basis for the relative timing of the sequence of the coming events. The heavenly Lady informed Conchita Gonzales of the date and time that the Great Miracle would take place at the grove of pine trees, located at the top of the bluff just outside the village of San Sebastian de Garabandal. This precise date was told privately to Conchita's mother and then to Pope Paul VI and Cardinal Ottaviani in 1966. All three of these persons are deceased, but it is very likely that Pope John Paul II and now Pope Benedict XVI have been informed of that date.

Conchita Gonzales disclosed publicly that the Great Miracle will occur on a Thursday evening at 8:30 PM in one of the months of March, April, or May and between the 8th and the 16th of that month. She included the 8th and 16th of the month in the range of dates. She said that it will last about 15 minutes and will be the greatest public Miracle in the history of the world.

Conchita has also made known that the Great Miracle will take place on a Church feast day of a saint identified in a special way with the Sacrament of the Eucharist. It seems that the saint was a martyr in a way related to the Eucharist. Conchita said the saint has an unusual name and was not Spanish.

Additional disclosures of Conchita are:

(1) The blind Joey Lomangino of New York will receive new eyes on the day of the Great Miracle. Joey was born in October of 1930. He lost his eyes in an accident in 1947.

(2) The pope will see the Great Miracle from wherever he is. It is assumed that Conchita was speaking about the pope of the time of the Miracle. Our Lady said at Garabandal that there would be four* more popes after Pope John XXIII, and then would come the "end of the times." She also indentified the event that would mark the "end of the times"; that event is the Warning which stops the Communist Tribulation and corrects the conscience of the world. Pope Benedict XVI, born in 1927, is the fourth pope after Pope John XXIII.

(3) The Franciscan monk, now Saint Padre Pio, will see the Great Miracle. Conchita was told this by the Lady from Heaven before her appearances at Garabandal ended on November 13, 1965. Saint Padre Pio died in 1968 and was canonized a saint in 2002. After he died, it was revealed to Conchita by a fellow monk that Padre Pio had seen the Miracle, in advance, and before he died.

(4) In the early days of the Events of Garabandal, the Virgin Mary spoke to the young girls about the reunification of the Churches that would come in the future. At some point during her apparitions in Garabandal, She said that a happy event would occur in the Church on the day of the Great Miracle.

(5) Conchita was told by the Blessed Virgin to publicly announce the day of the Miracle eight days prior.

(*It has been said that there would be three more popes after Pope John XXIII and then would come the end of the times. Clarity on this apparent discrepancy is explained in the German language book, *"Garabandal—the Finger of God"* by Albrecht Weber. In sum, Our Lady actually said there would be four more popes after Pope John XXIII, but She was not counting one of them, ostensibly John Paul I who died so quickly after he became pope.)

Mari Loli Mazon was told the year of the coming Universal Warning to the entire human race, which will precede the Great Miracle by no more than 12 months. She told some persons that the year of the Warning will be an even-numbered year. (Mari Loli died on April 20, 2009.)

The Lady from Heaven also revealed that the Universal Warning would not only change the conscience of the world but would stop the Great Tribulation of Communism, when things are at their worst. She also said that this Communist Tribulation will be very intense, will gain dominion of the whole world, but not be of a long duration.

Suddenly and Unexpectedly

It is interesting to note that Pope Benedict XVI ended his sermon at Fatima on May 13, 2010, with these words: ***"May the seven years which separate us from the centenary of the apparitions hasten the fulfillment of the prophecy of the triumph of the Immaculate Heart of Mary, to the glory of the Most Holy Trinity."***

The pope was referring to the apparitions of Our Lady at Fatima in 1917, who said back then: *"The good will be martyred; the Holy Father will have much to suffer; various nations will be annihilated. In the end, my Immaculate Heart will triumph. The Holy Father will consecrate Russia to me, and she shall be converted, and a period of peace will be granted to the world."*

At Garabandal on July 10, 1963, while giving thanks-giving after receiving Holy Communion, Conchita had a dialogue with Jesus, though He was not visible to her.

Conchita asked Him: *"Why is the Miracle coming?.. To convert many people?"*

Jesus answered: *"To convert the whole world."*

Conchita: *"Will Russia be converted?"*

Jesus: *"It also will be converted; and so everyone will love Our Hearts."* ["Our Hearts" = the Hearts of Jesus and Mary.]

Catholic readers who doubt that God could effect the rapid restoration of the Church in Russia after a papal consecration might ponder the words of St. Padre Pio, one of the greatest saints of modern times and a great promoter of the Fatima message. When asked if Russia will be converted to the Catholic Faith, as Our Lady of Fatima promised through Sr. Lucia, Padre Pio said that it will be, and suddenly, to the surprise of many. But then he added: "And Russia will give America a good example of what it means to convert." Padre Pio promised that the U.S.A. would also convert to the Catholic Faith, but that its conversion would happen gradually.* The saint's words confirm that the purpose of the consecration of Russia is to set her apart to be a light to the nations, including the United States, and that her "conversion" to the Catholic Faith does not mean the adoption of Latin Christianity but rather the full realization of her Eastern Christian heritage under the universal fatherhood and magisterial authority of the successor of St. Peter. (*"Padre Pio and America" by Frank Rega)

If the final sentence of Pope Benedict's Sermon at Fatima on Thursday, May 13, 2010, is a sign of the time of the Triumph of the Immaculate Heart of Mary (see page 107). If what the pope hopes for does occur that could very well be when Russia is converted. If so, that would seem to be also the time of the Great Miracle at Garabandal, because Jesus said that following the Miracle, Russia would be converted. There has been conjecture by people, who have known Conchita well, that April will be the month of the Miracle in whatever year the Miracle actually occurs.

October 13, 1884: Pope Leo XIII finished offering Holy Mass at 12 noon. As he was leaving the altar area, he suddenly turned around and looked intently at a vision above the tabernacle for 12 minutes. When the vision ended he went immediately to the sacristy and wrote the now familiar prayer to St. Michael the Archangel which we pray seeking his protection. The original prayer was longer than the one normally said now.

When the Pope was asked what he saw, he explained that he saw a vision of a conversation between the devil and God the Father in which the devil bragged that He could destroy the Catholic Church. God the Father told the devil that he would allow him 100 years, and no more, to try.

Since, neither the Pope nor anyone else knew for sure when the 100-year period would begin, there have been various speculations about the beginning date. Some thought it may have begun the day that the Pope had the vision; others thought it might be the year 1900. And others have independently arrived at the likelihood that the 100-year period began in 1917, when Mary made her six famous apparitions at Fatima, predicting in advance the great Miracle of the Sun, which did occur precisely as predicted on October 13, 1917. At least 70,000 people saw the great Miracle of the Sun. October 13, 1917 was precisely 33 years to the date following Pope Leo XIII's vision. At Fatima, Mary warned that from Russia would rise atheistic Communism with all its errors and destruction, and She gave the remedies to overcome it—remedies that have not been adequately or properly applied. Shortly after the Miracle of the Sun, Russia did give rise to atheistic Communism and the Battle between the Woman clothed with the Sun and the Red Dragon became decisively dramatic in our times.

April 13, 2017, is a Thursday. In 2017, it will be the common Holy Thursday for the Catholics and the Orthodox. It is also the feast day of St. Hermenegild who died as a martyr of the Eucharist (according to the Church calendar when this is being written in 2012). He was 22 years old when martyred.

One day when Conchita was still quite young, while sitting at a table among some people in Garabandal, she suddenly related what seemed to be a vision of another young martyr of the Eucharist whom, she said at that time, was the one whose feast day would be on the day of the future Great Miracle. The description she gave of his martyrdom was easily discerned by the people around Conchita to be St. Tarcisius, but when the people mentioned that name, Conchita had no reaction. He died in the Third Century, A.D. His feast day is celebrated on August 15th, but, since that day is occupied by the Solemnity of the Assumption of Mary, he is not mentioned in the General Roman Calendar, but only in the Roman Martyrology. If St. Tarcisius is the saint whose feast day occurs on the same day of the Great Miracle, it seems that the Church would have to change the calendar date of his feast to an eligible date for the Miracle in the spring of the year.

These are mysterious things, which Divine Wisdom holds in secret until the time willed by God. Conchita was told that she was to announce the date of the Miracle eight days in advance. I now have reason to believe that it is the wish of God that we not try to figure out the precise date of the coming Great Miracle. It seems that one of many good reasons for the mystery about the precise time of future predicted events is to confuse false prophets, preventing them from glorifying themselves by "stealing" accurate information concerning future events.

Only God has true knowledge of the future. We were given sufficient information to know the sequence of the major coming events and what they are. This will be a comfort to those who know these things, even now, but especially during the time of the Communist Tribulation.

Back to the sequence of the unpredecented, major events that Mary, Queen of Prophets, gave to the young girls of Garabandal: The sequence is first—the coming of the "sudden and unexpected" Great Tribulation of Communism led by Russia. The <u>second</u> is the Great, Universal Warning to all mankind, which stops the Communist Tribulation and corrects the conscience of the world. The <u>third</u> is the Great Miracle to occur within 12 months following the Warning and to take place on a Thursday evening in one of the months of March, April, or May in some future year.

Reversing this sequence we see that the Warning must occur within 12 months prior to the Great Miracle. Since the Warning stops the Communist Tribulation, the Tribulation must begin prior to the Warning. The terrible Communist Tribulation is said to be of great intensity but of a relatively short duration. Could Communism gain dominion of the whole world in perhaps two years or less? Considering the technology of today, it seems quite possible.

As already noted, only Conchita knows the date of the Great Miracle, and possibly Pope Benedict XVI, who is the last pope of our times. Nevertheless, as this book is being written in 2012, the signs are everywhere that the current structure of human society is rapidly disintegrating—a dynamic condition which would make it easy for the "Scourge of God," Russia, to lead Communism to "suddenly and unexpectedly" wreak havoc, death and destruction everywhere and gain 'dominion of the whole world."

Suddenly and Unexpectedly

It was written earlier in this book that the Warning will stop the Communist Tribulation and that the Warning will mark the end of our times. It will also correct the conscience of the world. I have been informed more than once that Mari Loli has said to some persons that the Warning will come in an even-numbered year.

Readers of this book have an abundance of information about the major events of the very last days of our times and should recognize the nearness of these terrible things to occur. They should also know that the survivors of these events will enjoy the times of a relatively "short" period of peace after the Great Miracle and later the "long" period of heavenly peace after the Chastisement of Fire.

As noted above, the Virgin Mary revealed at Garabandal that the Warning marks the End of the Times. She also gave information about the popes which leads to the understanding that Pope Benedict XVI is the last pope before the end of our times. It is possible that he could be killed during the Communist Tribulation.* He was born in April of 1927. As pointed out above, blind Joey Lomangino was born in October of 1930. He is to receive new eyes on the day of the Great Miracle. His blindness, due to the loss of his eyes, resulted from an accident in 1947 while he was changing a truck tire at his father's ice house.

(*-See note on page 96, which refers to his resignation.)

93

What about the Chastisement of Fire from Heaven? When will it come? We were told at Garabandal that it would come after the Great Miracle, but no precise time was given. It seems that the Chastisement of Fire from Heaven will come at some point between the "certain period of peace" that God will grant following the Triumph of the Immaculate Heart of Mary and the long reign of peace that follows the Chastisement. However, there is an interesting indicator in the literature on Garabandal that is worth considering concerning the timing of the coming Chastisement. It has to do with the agonizing cries of the young girls of Garabandal, who were shown the Great Chastisement of Fire from Heaven during the second night of screams on June 20, 1962, as described in Chapter Four.

As the girls were screaming, one of them, Mari Loli, shouted: *"Wait, wait. Take the little children first. Give everyone a chance to confess!. . ."* The Virgin Mary responded that by the time it came, they would all be adults. The little children of that day are now in their fifties as this book is being written in 2012.

While writing this book, the author had a conversation in June of 2012 with a Priest who had spoken with Maximina, the aunt of Conchita of Garabandal, who told him that Our Lady had told Conchita that at some point after the Great Miracle people would revert toward evil again. Conchita apparently understood from this that the Chastisement of Fire from Heaven would certainly come.

This accords with what has been said by Our Lord to an Italian mystic of impeccable reputation and great holiness. The conclusion is simple: After the conversion of Russia and the unification of the churches and the "certain period of peace" predicted at Fatima, there will be a reversion of society toward evil, to which God will exercise his Justice with the Great Chastisement of Fire.

From the pool of persons whom God chooses to survive the Chastisement of Fire from Heaven, God will establish throughout the world the Kingdom of the Father's Will in souls as it was in the beginning in the Garden of Eden. This will bring the long period of real peace, harmony and happiness, and the purpose of the Divine Will for creating man will be fulfilled. The Will of God will at last be done and lived as It is in Heaven. There will be no exercising of Divine Justice during this period. All will be Mercy, and the only laws will be Truth and Love. More details on this will be given in Chapter Ten and Chapter Eleven.

It was revealed at Garabandal that there is a spiritual coming of Jesus and that the people of the new era will live for God until the end of time.

Note: The Virgin Mary's reference at Garabandal to a "spiritual coming of Jesus" seems to conform to statements by some of the

Church Fathers and echoed by St. Bernard of Clairvaux that there will be a "hidden coming of Christ" before the visible coming of Christ on Judgment Day at the end of time. This "spiritual coming" or "hidden coming" of Christ conforms to the doctrine of living in the Divine Will, made known in the *"Book of Heaven,"* by which Jesus, using the humanities of his children on earth, lives really in them His Divine Life. These souls freely offer themselves to become living hosts, to possess the same Life of Jesus within them as in the Eucharist. This is the manner in which Jesus comes and reigns on earth in His saints in the time of the Kingdom of peace on earth as in Heaven—the time of "one fold and one shepherd" (Jn: 10, 16)

This way of Christ's coming would be more beneficial to souls of men than His visible, physical coming in His natural mode of existence, because souls would not merely see and touch Him, but would possess Him truly alive within them, with innumerable, spiritual and eternal benefits among which is that He will live the enrapturing and fascinating Life of the HolyTrinity in them as He does in Heaven. He will animate and direct all that they do, think and say, transforming all their activity into divine, eternal, and infinite operations, thus fulfilling the very purpose for which God created man—even as it was in the beginning of human history before Adam did his own will and withdrew from his original, intimate relationship with God.

Resignation of Pope Benedict XVI:

On February 11, 2013, Pope Benedict XVI announced his resignation which would be effective at 8:00 PM on February 28, 2013. This confirms that his pontificate ends prior to the End of the Times, which Our Lady says will be marked by the Warning. On page 93, the author remarked that it is possible that Pope Benedict XVI could be killed during the Communist Tribulation which precedes the Warning. Now that he has resigned, his pontificate happily won't end that way. His successor will be the pope who will reign through the Communist Tribulation, the Warning (which stops that Tribulation) and the Miracle.

Chapter Nine

Fatima–Garabandal: One Story in Two Parts

The Virgin Mary, appeared at Garabandal more than 2,000 times during a period of four years and four months, fulfilling a promise She had made to the three shepherd children of Fatima on October 13, 1917—the day of the great Miracle of the Sun at Fatima. On that day in Fatima, dressed as Our Lady of Mt. Carmel and holding the Baby Jesus in her arms, She bade farewell to the three shepherd children saying, *"until San Sebastian, Spain"* (*"até Sao Sebastiao da Hesphana"*). This San Sebastian, Spain is not to be confused with the large city of San Sebastian at the coastal border with France on the Bay of Biscay. The San Sebastian, Spain that the Heavenly Lady spoke about is the tiny village of San Sebastian de Garabandal located in the Province of Cantabria in northern Spain.

This underlines a direct linkage between the two series of apparitions—Fatima and Garabandal; and the two can be called one story in two parts, separated by forty-four years.

A glaring and serious observation of this relationship between Fatima and Garabandal is the fact that Pope John XXIII did not reveal the Third Secret of Fatima in 1960 as Sr. Lucia had requested, saying: "...by that time, it will be more clearly understood," and, "...because the Blessed Virgin wishes it so," and the fact that Our Lady appeared the following year (1961) at San Sebastian, Spain as She had promised, and that her messages at San Sebastian de Garabandal, Spain are strongly indicative of what the Third Secret of Fatima likely contained in the yet undisclosed, handwritten part on one sheet of paper of 20-25 lines. That single sheet was described by Bishop João Pereira Venâncio in his story about the day he forwarded the Third Secret to Rome in 1957, although he did not actually read the words. The single sheet description is also supported by comments of Bishops working with Pope Pius XII, Pope John XXIII, Pope Paul VI, and Father Joaquin Alonso—official Fatima archivist for 16 years.

The Vatican's disclosure of the Third Secret of Fatima in the year 2,000 was taken from four sheets of paper—not one sheet—thus, much mystery! It seems from the investigative evidence that the four-sheet version was in one envelope and the one-sheet version was in another. The one-sheet version was kept in the Pope's bedroom; the other in the Holy Office archive.

There is not sufficient space here to write about the sincerity, humility and holiness of Bishop João Pereira Venâncio, mentioned above, but it is germane to this subject to point out that he said, "Garabandal is the continuation of Fatima." The whole drama of the apparitions of Our Lady of Mt. Carmel and St. Michael the Archangel at Garabandal is replete with instructions, messages both direct and indirect based on their actual words, their actions, marvelous occurrences, signs in the sky, as well as the actions of the four young girls to whom they appeared. There were many predictions made during the years of the apparitions (1961-1965) of things to come, many of which have already occurred. As of the time of this printing, the major predictions of unprecedented events are pending, however.

In her 1957 interview with Father Augustin Fuentes, Sister Lucia of Fatima stated, "Many times the Most Holy Virgin told my cousins* as well as myself, that many nations will disappear from the face of the earth, that Russia will be the instrument of chastisement chosen by Heaven to punish the whole world if we do not beforehand obtain the conversion of that poor nation..." [*the two other shepherd children to whom Our Lady appeared]

Non-Fiction

At Garabandal, the Virgin Mary said: "If we do not change, Communism will gain dominion of the whole world."

Points of Consideration which Demonstrate that Garabandal is Truly the Continuation of Fatima.

1. Our Lady's "Good-bye" to the children of Fatima. Dressed as Our Lady of Mt. Carmel with the Baby Jesus in her arms, She waved her farewell and said, "until San Sebastian, Spain." (*"até Sao Sebastiao da Hesphana"*)

2. Our Lady at Fatima did not refrain from showing innocent young children a terrifying vision of Hell, where the damned souls were seen screaming as they were being tossed about in the flames of eternal fire. At Garabandal, Our Lady did not refrain from showing the innocent, young girls the terrifying, bloody Tribulation of Communism to come, or the flames of the flesh-consuming Fire of the Great Chastisement to come if people resume Godless lives after the Miracle of Garabandal.

Vision of Hell at Fatima: Lucia, the oldest of the three shepherd children, said, "As Our lady spoke these words she opened her hands once more, as she had done during the two previous months. The rays of light seemed to penetrate the earth, and we saw as it were a sea of fire. Plunged in this fire were demons and souls in human form, like transparent burning embers, all blackened or burnished bronze, floating about in the conflagration, now raised into the air by the flames that issued from within themselves together with great clouds of smoke, now flowing back on every side like sparks in huge fires, without weight or equilibrium, amid shrieks and groans of pain and despair, which horrified us and made us tremble with fear. (It must have been this sight which caused me to cry out, as people say they heard me do.) The demons could be distinguished by their terrifying and repellant likeness to frightful and unknown animals, black and transparent like burning coals. Terrified and as if to plead for succor, we looked up at Our Lady, who said to us, so kindly and so sadly:

"You have seen Hell, where the souls of poor sinners go. It is to save them that God wants to establish in the world devotion to my Immaculate Heart. If you do what I tell you, many souls will be saved, and there will be peace. This war will end, but if men do not refrain from offending God, another and more terrible war will begin during the pontificate of Pius XI. When you see a night that is lit by a strange and unknown light [This occurred on January 28, 1938, in the reign of Pope Pius XI], you will know it is the sign God gives you that He is about to punish the world with war and with hunger, and by the persecution of the Church and the Holy Father."

At Garabandal Conchita said, "If we do not change, the Chastisement will be terrible, in keeping with what we deserve. We saw it, but I cannot say what it consists of because I do not have permission from the Blessed Virgin to do so.... When I saw it, I felt a very great fear, and that notwithstanding that I was looking at the Blessed Virgin at the same time."

Note the similarities between the vision of Hell at Fatima and the vision of the future Chastisment of Fire at Garabandal. (see page 75)

3.   At Fatima, Our Lady said that *in the end* the pope will consecrate Russia to her Immaculate Heart and that Russia will be converted. At Garabandal Our Lord told Conchita in a locution that as a result of the Miracle of Garabandal, Russia would be converted.

Thus, it seems that at some point a pope will finally consecrate Russia, by name, to the Immaculate Heart of Mary and do so with the Bishops. One of the Fatima experts says that the conversion of Russia means conversion to the Catholic Church.

The Garabandal predictions also indicate the same thing.

> **Note:** An exhaustive amount of research has been done by honorable persons in various places, and they have well demonstrated that the proper and necessary consecration of Russia, by name, to the Immaculate Heart of Mary has not yet been done.

4. Bishop Venancio of Leiria, Portugal, who handled the Third Secret of Fatima when it was given to the papal legate to take to Rome in 1957, said unequivocally "Garabandal is the continuation of Fatima."

5. In both Fatima and Garabandal, Our Lady warned about Russia and Communism.

At Fatima, She spoke about Russia and Communism and all the evils that would ensue. She said that Russia will be the instrument of chastisement chosen by Heaven to punish the whole world. She also gave the remedies for preventing that horrendous evil, but the remedies failed to be administered sufficiently and properly.

At Garabandal, She spoke many times about Communism: that it would come back, that it would be led by Russia and cause a very great Tribulation, and that Russia would gain dominion of the whole world. She did not talk about Islamic Jihadism.

At this point remarks about just a few of the notable persons who have affirmed their belief in Garabandal are in order.

1. **St. Padre Pio (1887-1968)** saw the Great Miracle in advance, confirmed by Father Bernardino Cennamo, O.F.M., Cap. Joachim Bouflet, Ph.D. (Univ. of Paris, 1972) tells a story about going to Confession to the (now) Saint Padre Pio in July of 1968. Padre Pio told him: "Consecrate yourself to the Virgin of Carmel who appeared at Garabandal." When Mr. Bouflet responded, "So its true?" [i.e. the events of Garabandal] Padre Pio replied, *"Certo e vero!"* (Certainly it is true!)

And here is what St. Padre Pio wrote at the end of a letter to Conchita of Garabandal: *"I give you only one counsel: Pray and make others pray, because the world is at the beginning of perdition. They do not believe in you or in your conversations with the Lady in White . . . They will believe when it will be too late."*

In January of 1966, Conchita, accompanied by her mother and another lady had an opportunity to visit Padre Pio (now Saint Padre Pio) in his little room at the Monastery, "Our Lady of Grace," in San Giovanni Rotundo, Italy. During that visit, Padre Pio told Conchita that the future, great Miracle at Garabandal will be paid for by the blood of the Europeans—oceans of blood.

2.   St. Maria Maravillas (1891-1974) warned Bishop Puchol Montis, one of the former bishops of Santander, Spain, that he would have a sudden death, which did happen as a result of an automobile accident on May 8, 1967. Bishop Montis seems to have opposed the events of Garabandal irresponsibly in a manner unworthy of his office.

3.   Bishop João Venancio (1904-1985) of Leira, Portugal. He is the Bishop who turned over the famous Third Secret of Fatima to the papal legate in 1957. Bishop Venancio said that Garabandal was the continuation of Fatima. He described the Third Secret of Fatima as 20 to 24 lines, handwritten on a single sheet of paper, which contrasts with the four sheets of the Third Secret revealed by the Vatican in the year 2000. It seems there were two versions or two separate parts of the secret. One was kept at a special office adjoining the Vatican. The other, the single sheet, was kept in a desk in the pope's bedroom.

4.   Fr. Luis Andreu, S.J. (1925-1961) saw the Great Miracle in advance at 8:30 PM on August 8, 1961. He said that this was the happiest day of his life, that we should never fear the supernatural, that we should imitate the attitude of the little girls of Garabandal towards their

Heavenly Mother, and then died in a state of quiet joy a little later, in the early hours of August 9, 1961.

5.   Blessed Mother Theresa of Calcutta (1910-1997) was a firm believer in Garabandal and devloped a bond of friendship with Conchita and Jacinta of the Garabandal events.

6.   Venerable Mother Esperanza (1893-1983), was a stigmatist and founder of two religious orders dedicated to the Merciful Love of God. She also advised high dignitaries of the Church who went to her for counsel. She, too, believed in Garabandal.

7.   Pope Paul VI (1897-1978) Already mentioned in Chapter Two are the following references to Pope Paul VI's attitude toward Garabandal: Pope Paul VI referred to what happened during those years at Garabandal with these words: "It is the most beautiful story of humanity since the days of Christ. It is like a second life of the Virgin on earth. And we can never be grateful enough for it." In 1966, when Conchita, then 17 years old, was called to Rome by Cardinal Ottaviani, the Pope met her and those with her and said to her, "Conchita, I bless you and with me the whole Church will bless you."

When Pope Paul VI learned that Fr. Luis Andreu's Mother was to take her permanent vows as a Visitandine nun, he contacted the superiors of the surviving three, priest brothers of Fr. Luis to get their permission to let the brothers attend the ceremonies of their mother's vows. The pope also personally paid for one of the brother's round-trip air fare from Taiwan.

Fr. Luis is the Priest who died of joy shortly after seeing the coming Great Miracle in advance on August 8, 1961, at Garabandal. After his death, his widowed mother entered the relgious life as a cloistered nun.]

8. **Blessed Pope John Paul II** (1920-2005) There are several signs of Pope John Paul II's belief in Garabandal, but one that is significant is that in the year 2000, after reading the German book, *"Garabandal—the Finger of God"* the Holy Father, asked his secretary, Mons. Dziwisz (now Cardinal Dziwisz) to write to its author as follows:

"May God reward you for everything, especially for the deep love with which you are making the events connected with Garabandal more widely known. May the Message of the Mother of God find an entrance into hearts before it is too late. As an expression of joy and gratitude, the Holy Father gives you his apostolic blessing." Then, below Mons. Dziwisz's signature, Pope John Paul II wrote a personal note in his own handwriting and signed it.

In the latter part of Pope John Paul II's pontificate, the Vatican gave permission to the Bishop of Santander, Spain, to erect a basilica at Garabandal. The bishop at that time, Bishop Jose Villaplano, disdained the permission.

Pope John Paul II spoke about the The Greatest Confrontation in History before he became pope, saying:

"We are now standing in the face of the greatest historical confrontation humanity has gone through. I do not think that wide circles of the American society or wide circles of the Christian community realize this fully. We are now facing the final confrontation between the Church and the anti-Church, of the Gospel and the anti-Gospel. This confrontation lies within the plans of divine providence. It is a trial which the whole Church... must take up."

(Karol Cardinal Wojtyla, November 9, 1976—two years before becoming Pope John Paul II)

9. **Pope Benedict XVI** (born April 1927) A Priest whom the author knows and who lives in the Vatican has affirmed that Pope Benedict XVI believes in Garabandal. The last sentence of his sermon in Fatima on Thursday, May 13, 2010 is as follows:

"May the seven years which separate us from the centenary of the apparitions [of 1917 at Fatima] hasten the fulfillment of the prophecy of the triumph of the Immaculate Heart of Mary, to the glory of the Most Holy Trinity."

Should we ask: Does this pope know when to expect the Triumph of the Immaculate Heart of Mary (in her role as the Woman at battle with the red dragon for the souls of her children on earth)? Seven years from 2010 is 2017. Our Lady at Fatima said, "In the end, my Immaculate Heart will triumph, Russia will be converted and God would grant humanity a "certain period of peace."

107

At Garabandal, Jesus told Conchita that the purpose of the coming Great Miracle is to convert the whole world, that Russia will be converted and all will come to love "our Hearts" [i.e. the Sacred Heart of Jesus and the Immaculate Heart of Mary]. Comparing what Mary said at Fatima about the conversion of Russia and what Jesus said at Garabandal about the conversion of Russia, it is not unreasonable to thoughtfully consider that Russia's conversion will occur in connection with the year of the Great Miracle, and thus the Great Miracle should point to the Triumph of the Immaculate Heart, which this pope may be hinting will take place in 2017. If so, the predictions of the Communist Tribulation, the Warning, the Great Miracle, the End of these Times will occur very, very soon. If the pope's words at the end of his sermon in Fatima are not indicators of the year of the Triumph of the Immaculate Heart, then we may have just a little more time.

(Note: The precise timing of these predicted events is subject to moderated speculation, but not so—the events themselves.)

10.   Antonio Ruffini: The author has read that this man was a stigmatist in Rome, Italy, and a friend of Pope Pius XII. According to Rev. Paul Kramer, who knew him for 20 years, Ruffini was asked in his home in the 1990's: "Is John Paul II the Pope who is going to do the Consecration of Russia?" He answered: "No, it's not John Paul II. It will not be his immediate successor either, but the one after that. He is the one who will consecrate Russia."

Suddenly and Unexpectedly

(It is usual for authentic stigmatists to have other mystical gifts—often the gift of prophecy.)

11.   Father Malachi Martin (1921-1999) worked closely with popes John XXIII and Paul VI. He said that he had read the Third Secret of Fatima. Being interviewed on the Art Bell Show in 1997, he stated: "… everything will be finished in less than twenty years." He was speaking of the genre of future events written about in this book.

12.   Joey Lomangino (born October 1930). Joey lost both eyes in an accident in 1947. He visited Padre Pio in the early 1960's and then went to Garabandal. He met Conchita, who was told by the Virgin Mary to write to Joey and tell him that he will receive new eyes on the day of the Great Miracle and see permanently*. Joey has successfully spread the message of Garabandal throughout the world.

[*The precise meaning of the term, "permanently" —translated from the Spanish "para siempre"—is unclear, and can be rightfully subject to pious speculation due to many mysteries of the future, related to the Great Miracle and the beyond.]

13.   Fr. Walter Cizek, S.J. (1904-1984) Fr. Cizek, a firm believer in Garabandal, is known for his clandestine missionary work in Russia, beginning in 1939. He was eventually captured by the Russian Army and spent 15 years in confinement and hard labor. Five of those years was spent in the harsh Lubyanka Prison. He returned to

America after his release in 1963.   Fr. Cizek's cause for beatification and canonization has been introduced.

A Few More Interesting Points

One day during the apparitions, Mary Loli asked Our Lady about how the human race was formed. Our Lady answered that we did not descend from a monkey, or by evolution, or by any animal but from a perfect man, Adam. Our Lady also said that man had been created on earth just as he is today.

[**Note:** Our Lady obviously was referring here to our human nature and not to the state of our souls following Original Sin. In other words, we have not slowly evolved from animals and so-called man-like "pre-Adamites."]

Our Lady predicted the confusion that would come after Vatican Council II, but She in no way blamed the Council.   Remember the Second Formal Message at Garabandal–June 18, 1965.

The Great Miracle that God will perform at Garabandal at 8:30 PM on a Thursday in the Spring of some future year will be the greatest public miracle since the creation of the world. During the Miracle we will see the **Glory of God** but won't die from seeing this due to a special preventative grace. The sick will be cured, and unbelievers will believe. There was a lady, now deceased, who worked with Fr. Laffineur investigating the events of Garabandal from the start. The two recorded thousands of testimonies and documentation reports, including a dialogue between

Suddenly and Unexpectedly

Conchita and Our Lady, which was tape-recorded with Our Lady's voice audible on the tape. This same lady said that during the Great Miracle, people will have a sensible experience of the Indwelling Trinity. [Apparently one would have to be in the state of grace.] She also said that Priests who are there would not only have that experience but would also have a sensible experience of the active presence of Our Lord in them as during the Consecration of the communion host at Mass.

At the time of the Great Miracle the Spanish Military will generously support the sick coming to Garabandal and nothing negative will happen to them.

There will be a very happy event in the Church on the very same day of the Miracle but not associated directly with it. In the future the various religions will unite. Divisions will cease, etc.

———————

Non-Fiction

Chapter Ten

The Renewal of
The Face of the Earth
and the
Happy and Holy Times to Come

At Fatima, Portugal, in 1917, Our Lady, appeared to the three shepherd children, and She told them that in the end (of the terrible events that She predicted to come) her Immaculate Heart would triumph and God would grant humanity a "certain period of peace."

Made known at Fatima in 1917 was the very imminent Bolshevik Revolution and the terrible effects of Communism, which would be spread by Russia. Our Lady of Fatima had predicted the evils of Communism, the loss of Faith, the **annihilation of nations**, and She added that in the end the pope will consecrate Russia to her Immaculate Heart, that Russia will be converted and a **certain period of peace** *will be granted to the world.*

This Warning from Heaven also provided the remedies for stopping this evil at both the papal and hierarchical level as well as at the level of all the faithful, but the remedy at the papal and hierarchical level was never applied in the precise manner requested by God. Insufficient has been the application at the level of all the faithful. At the papal and hierarchical level, the Queen of Heaven, sent by God, requested that the Pope consecrate Russia (by name) to the Immaculate Heart of Mary in union with all the Bishops. At the level of all the faithful, She requested the daily recitation of the Rosary; the establishment of the First Five Saturday devotions; devotion to Her Immaculate Heart; a prayerful life; penance and amendment of life. These requests remain ever relevant and urgent. And we must continue to heed Her maternal warnings.

It was also made known that if these requests of God were not fulfilled, another World War would come in the Reign of Pope Pius XI (the name of this future pope was actually given in 1917). The oldest of the young shepherds, Lucia dos Santos, was given a Secret, which was to be opened by the pope in 1960. In 1960, the envelope containing this famous "Third Secret" was opened by Pope John XXIII, but was not made public as many had hoped. There is much mystery about all of this, including the two envelopes—one kept in the Holy Office, the other in the pope's bedroom, which have been written about in various books.

Other very reliable prophecies, biblical and otherwise, speak of a *long period of peace and harmony*.

Thus, it seems that there will be two periods of peace—one will be relatively short and the other will be a long and perfect one. The first will follow the Great Miracle predicted at Garabandal. The second will follow the Great Chastisement of Fire from Heaven after the relatively short period of peace.

For the survivors of the Great Tribulation of Communism, which will soon be followed by the Great Miracle at Garabandal, the first period of peace should last about 25 years, based on part of the message given at La Salette, France, in 1846, by Our Lady to Melanie Calvat and Maximin Girard. During this "certain period peace" it seems that there will be much evangelization of the Gospel that Jesus gave us while He was on earth and great numbers of conversions to the Catholic Church. There will also be considerable evangelization of the Gospel of the Kingdom of the Divine Will, which is none other than the necessary explanation and fulfillment of great mysteries hidden in the Lord's Prayer and which are now being unveiled by an extraordinary act of Divine Providence predestined for these times.

Unfortunately, it appears that there will be a moral retrogression toward the end of the "certain period of peace" leading into the times of the rise and fall of the

Anti-Christ, according to some sources. The divine displeasure will be so great that Divine Justice will have no other option than to cleanse the world to make it a proper place for the Father's Kingdom to reign on earth in fulfillment of the Lord's Prayer, so that His Will be lived and done as His Will is lived and done in Heaven, where all possess one Will—the Divine Will—which animates, directs and reigns in all: God, his Angels, and his Saints.

The Long and Glorious Period of Peace

God's Plan for Mankind—The Father's Kingdom in Souls

Let us begin this very important part with some words from the new Catechism of the Catholic Church. Article One of Chapter Two of the Catechism is titled "The Revelation of God " and the first section of this Article is titled "God Reveals His 'Plan of Loving Goodness.'"

This is what the Catechism says: "It pleased God, in his goodness and wisdom, to reveal Himself and to make known the mystery of his Will. His Will was that men should have access to the Father, through Christ, the Word made flesh, in the Holy Spirit, and thus become sharers in the Divine Nature."

"God, who 'dwells in unapproachable light,' wants to communicate his own Divine Life to the men He freely created, in order to adopt them as his sons in his only-begotten Son..."

What follows is based upon what is made known in the *"Book of Heaven"* written over a period of 40 years by the Servant of God, Luisa Piccarreta, whose mission was to let God work out his eternal plan that would make her his herald of a new era for mankind in which the Lord's Prayer is brought to fulfillment: "Fiat Voluntas Tua" –"Thy Will be done" —on earth as in Heaven.

I. God, Eternity and the Divine Will

Eternity is an immense circle without beginning and without end. And in this circle is found the Kingdom of God, without beginning or end, where the Most Holy Trinity possesses infinite happiness, riches and beauty, harmony and joys, beatitude and delights.

Now, this Kingdom where God exists is the Kingdom of the Divine Will. This Kingdom is everything for God. It is uncreated; It is eternal; and It produces all that God is and all that God does. All this is done in one, single, uninterrupted Act. And this single Act produces innumerable effects both within the Trinity and outside the Trinity. The circumference of this single Act of the Divine

Will is so immense that nothing can flee from It. It embraces everyone and everything all at once; and everything comes from that Prime Act of God as a single Act. Thus Creation, Redemption and Sanctification are one, single Act of the Three Divine Persons.

The most beautiful, most sublime and wonderful thing to be said of the Holy Trinity—Father, Son and Holy Spirit— is that They all Three possess one, same Will; and all their Divine Activity is produced by that one Divine Will. Therefore, there is always and forever total and perfect Peace, Harmony, Unity, Happiness and ever new Joys among the Three Divine Persons.

From this One Divine Will is born Divine Love. The Divine Will is the very Life of Divine Love. The Father eternally generates his Son by the Divine Intellect and Will, manifesting and communicating all that He is to his Beloved Son. And the Son, consumed in Divine Love for his Father, manifests and communicates to his Father his whole Self. And this mutual manifestation and communication of God to God is God! It is the Holy Spirit!

The Divine Will is the Life of the very Nature of God, and this Nature is all Divine Love in action, eternally and universally.

So, we can see that the Divine Will is the ALL of God Himself. The Divine Will is pure, uncreated Light. It is the animator and director of the Divine Being. It is the very Holiness of God and producer of all his attributes and perfections. Only that activity which is produced by the Divine Will attracts the Eye of the Father and fascinates and enraptures the Three Divine Persons.

The Divine Will alone produces what is most perfect and most pleasing to God. This Divine Will is the very fountain of all perfection, of all that is Holy, of all that is True, Beautiful, and Good.

II. Creation

God is complete and perfect in Himself. His happiness is also perfect; and the Three Divine Persons enjoy this happiness and contentment among Themselves in limitless seas of delight, having no absolute need of anything outside of Themselves.

But God's Nature is Love, and this Divine Love has the need to give. The Divine Love is the first-born Child of the Divine Will. And this Divine Love is so immense, so intense that it is compelled, so to speak, to go outside of the Trinity, manifesting and communicating itself but to whom?

Behold Creation! And man would be the primary object of this Creation. With the creation of man, Divine Love could find an outlet, a vessel into which to pour itself with all its infinite blessings and goods.

Therefore, man was designed by his Creator in a most perfect manner and with a most perfect plan to satisfy Divine Love and to glorify the Father in the most perfect possible way. In this beautiful plan of the Creator, man would be able to receive all that God can give; for God's Nature is to give all without holding anything back. (Those who do not know this, do not know God.) But God is infinite, and man is finite. So, what does Infinite Wisdom do?

Although man has his beginning in time, he has no beginning in God for God has always known man and has always loved him with infinite and eternal Love. The Divine Love designed man in such a way that men could be perfect created members of the Divine Family, sharing one same Life and animating principle with the Holy Trinity in perfect unity. In this Holy Plan of Divine Love, man, God's predilect creature, would have the capability of receiving Divine Love with all the infinite benefits, blessings and riches that a God can give. And man, in turn, would give perfect glory to the Father in all his thoughts, words and actions.

In this marvelous plan of the good God, man would have a body and a soul; and this soul would have three principle powers: will, intellect and memory. But, then, the

Creator would crown His beloved creatures with something Divine and unspeakably Holy. Man would be crowned with the Gift of the Divine Will, which would direct and animate all his activity, just as It directs and animates the activity of God Himself. In this manner, man would glorify the Father perfectly, returning Divine Love for Divine Love. Man would adore his God, thanking and blessing him with a Divine Will! And this Divine Will, given to man, would provide him with the capacity to receive the Torrents of Divine Love, Holiness, Graces and surprises which God wished to give him!

God wished to make man as holy as Himself and share one, same Life. Therefore, man's human will would be absorbed and unified with the Reigning and operating Divine Will, co-sharing in the eternal and universal activity of the Three Divine Persons. This was the only purpose of Creation: that the Infinite Love of the Blessed Trinity be fully communicated to man; and man, in turn, would love, glorify, adore, praise and thank his Creator with a Divine Will not of himself alone, but in and for all the things that God had created for love of man.

Rational man would disperse himself in the Divine Will, entering into all created things, giving them a voice speaking words of Divine Love to the Creator.

The acts of each human person were all prepared by the Creator. Each act was designed to give the Holy

Trinity perfect glory. Each person's page was written in the Book of Life with so much Divine Love, to be faithfully copied during each one's sojourn on earth.

And this was the *First Fiat of God*: Creation.

III. The Original State of Justice of Adam and Eve

Adam and Eve were the first human beings whom God placed on earth. God created their souls from nothing. Adam's body was fashioned from the dust of the earth, and the Lord God breathed into him a living soul. Eve's body was built from one of Adam's ribs. Although Adam and Eve had no physical existence before their creation in time, they always existed in the uncreated Mind of the Eternal God and were loved by Him with a divine and everlasting Love.

We ask: "What did Adam and Eve do to deserve existence? What did they do to deserve intelligence? What did they do to deserve to be images of the Almighty God and to even possess his Likeness? What did they do to deserve the special creation of Sanctifying Grace? And, above all, what did they do to deserve the uncreated, Supreme Gift of the Divine Will fountain of all Grace and all that is True, Beautiful, and Good?"

The Answer: NOTHING !! They did nothing to deserve all these gifts and blessings.

God wanted it, and so it all happened!

The Lord God wanted Adam and Eve to exist: therefore, they came into existence. God wanted them to have intelligence, free will, and an immortal soul. He wanted to make them to his own image and to possess his Likeness. He wanted them to possess the very Life of God Himself —the Divine Will. And so it all came to be just as God wanted it to be. And this was the Original State of Justice. Adam and Eve possessed and lived in the Divine Will.

Our first parents came from God as perfect creatures. They were created immaculate, and they possessed the Divine Will Itself, which reigned freely in their souls and bodies, directing and animating all their activity. This Gift of Original Justice, living in the Divine Will, made it possible for them to receive the full torrents of Divine Love and made them capable of returning Divine Love to their Creator. In this Original State they were created members of the Divine Family, sharing one common Life and Activity with the Father, Son , and Holy Spirit.

God crowned Adam and Eve as king and queen of Creation. With the Divine Will reigning in them, they could diffuse themselves in God, co-acting with Him in his universal activity.

The very Angels were stupified to see the Divine Will reigning and operating in those human creatures. What exalted privileges Adam and Eve had! The Original State of Justice was immeasurably sublime, holy and happy. Our first parents possessed God, and God possessed them. They were masterpieces of Creative Wisdom and Love.

IV. Original Sin

Everything was perfect in the beginning of human history. A perfect God created two perfect humans in a state of perfect unity of the human will with the Divine Will. All was peace and harmony between God and his beloved creatures; and God was enraptured in seeing his very own Activity emanating from every action of Adam and Eve. God and creature enjoyed mutual reciprocity of Divine Love.

Our first parents had a most holy duty to preserve themselves in the Original State in which their Creator had placed them. They had the solemn duty to always recognize and acknowledge their own nothingness and absolute dependency upon their Creator. Their serious responsibility was to never break their sublime unity with the Holy Trinity by choosing to do their own will.

Behold the wisdom of the one Commandment that God gave Adam and Eve. The Lord God had given them everything, but He forbade them to touch the Tree of Knowledge of Good and Evil or to eat its fruit. By faithful obedience to this Commandment, Adam and Eve would always acknowledge their own nothingness and the absolute supremacy of their God who had given them everything; for the Gift of the Divine Will contains all that Eternity contains, and it is not possible for God to give a creature a greater Gift. This Commandment of God was the test that God wanted to confirm Adam's innocence, sanctity and happiness and to give him the right of command over all Creation. But Adam was not faithful in the test; and God could not trust him. Therefore, he lost his command, his innocence, and happiness; and it can be said that he turned the work of Creation upside down.

But oh! What a most horrible tragedy! What a most woeful thing happened with Adam and Eve! They failed their test, and all humanity inherited the lowly and pitiful state to which our first parents had fallen. Instead of inheriting the Kingdom of the Divine Will, we, their children, have inherited the miserable and sorrowful reign of the human will, the sole cause of all our evils.

In God's plan the human will and the Divine Will would operate in perfect unity. The Divine Will would be the strength, the prime movement, the support, the food, and the life of the human will. The creature, with its human will alone, is all vacillating, weak, inconstant and disordered.

So how did it come about that Adam and Eve lost their Original State of Justice? Satan, disguised as a fascinating serpent, deceived Eve with an impossible story. Eve was deceived because she continued to listen and failed to pray to God for an understanding of this serpent and his story or to call her husband to help her understand, as he had received God's commands directly, whereas she had received those commands indirectly through Adam. Eve did take and eat the attractive, yet forbidden, fruit. She wanted Adam to share in her daring act, for she was driven by the false promises of the serpent, Satan, who is a liar and a murderer.

Eve called Adam, and he came and listened to his spouse. He took delight in looking at the beautiful but forbidden fruit. And he took delight in hearing the words of Eve. He succumbed to pride. He moved his thoughts away from God and forgot how much God was loving him, and he stopped loving God above all things and took and ate of the forbidden fruit. At that instant both knew they were naked for the both lost the celestial light of the Divine Will that invested them. Instead of admonishing and correcting Eve and maintaining his most holy relationship with God, Adam lost his Great Treasure the Gift of the Divine Will. And so, all humanity was deprived of the inheritance which God had entrusted to our first parents. With the loss of the Gift of the Divine Will, the very fountain of Sanctifying Grace, our first parents also lost many other wonderful gifts of which the Divine Will is the unique cause.

If Adam had remained faithful to God and had not eaten the forbidden fruit, Satan would have been defeated, and humanity would not have inherited Original Sin. The children of Adam would have inherited the Gift of the Divine Will. All God's desire in creating man was that he possess and live the life of the Divine Will. And as man went about, living in and gaining more and more knowledge of the Divine Will, the Word would have come gloriously to earth in human flesh and lived among men for a period of time to complete his Life in them. In this way, after repeated acts in the Divine Will, and man forming the fullness of Divine Life in himself, the Word would find man similar to Himself. Then, at a certain point the Word Incarnate would have absorbed all humanity into Himself and all would have ascended triumphantly into the delights of Heaven.

Most sadly, this was not the way it happened. But the Great Mercy of the Lord God had compassion on poor, pitiful mankind. Redemption was decreed—the Second Fiat of God; and 4000 years later the Redeemer came through the Blessed Virgin Mary, and the Word was made Flesh as a suffering Redeemer and dwelled among us.

V. Redemption

Original Sin ruptured man's sublime relationship with God and upset the Divine Plan for man. The Father, it seems, would not receive the Perfect Glory due Him from every thought, word and action of every human creature. And so, having foreknown the Fall of Adam and Eve, it seems that God would not have gone ahead with the Creation of the human race nor the great and wondrous Universe where man would live.

But the infinite Love of the Divine Persons had a remedy for this sad situation. The Father could still receive all the Glory He deserved from all the acts of creatures whom He had wanted to create with so much Love. Behold the Fiat of Redemption and then the Third Fiat of God, Sanctification ("Thy Will be done on earth as in Heaven").

Since Adam had lost something Divine, the Gift of the Divine Will, neither a man nor an Angel could restore what had been lost. The required Redeemer would have to be Divine. The Son of God would become Incarnate. His Holy Name would be Jesus.

He would assume a human nature which would serve as a veil for the action of the Divine Will, while always remaining God. As the man-God, with the Divine Will always reigning in Him, directing and animating all his activity, never giving life to his human will, He would recover all that Adam had lost. Above all, He would regain the lost Gift of the Divine Will.

He did this by undertaking all stages of natural human activity as an infant, as a child, as an adolescent, as a young man, and as a mature man never giving life to his human will but always letting the Divine Will reign, directing and animating all his activity, whether eating, working, speaking, breathing, walking, preaching, suffering, or dying. In the eternal Will, he would redo everything of man.

And then, since Jesus' only thought was for the Glory of his Father, He made marvelous use of the Eternal, Divine Will (which is present to all that has existed, does exist, and will exist) to give the Father all the Perfect Glory which God had intended to receive from every human being, in their every thought, word, action and movement. In the Divine Will, He entered into every moment of everyone's life, from Adam to the last person to live on earth, redoing all thoughts, words, actions, etc., in the Divine Will just as they had been foreordained in God in Eternity in the Book of Life, where the page for each creature has been written with so much Divine Love.

Along with this great and prime purpose of regaining the lost Gift of the Divine Will, Jesus would reopen the gates of Heaven for mankind; and He would establish the Catholic Church and the Sacraments to provide Grace, and all the necessary means for humanity to arrive at that glorious day appointed by the Father when the Divine Will would reign once again on earth as in Heaven. The world can never come to an end until the Kingdom of the Divine Will is established in the souls of men, so that the Father's Will be done on earth as in Heaven.

Suddenly and Unexpectedly

The Mother of Jesus is the Virgin Mary, who was conceived without sin. She is the Immaculate Conception and, above all, She is the Mother and Queen of the Divine Will. Mary was created with the Kingdom of the Divine Will reigning in her body and soul. And this was most necessary for the Incarnation, for it would have been entirely unfitting for the Word to take flesh in her womb had He found the human will reigning in Her. Having established his Divine Kingdom in Her, even from the moment of her Immaculate Conception, the Divine King found a worthy dwelling place to become Incarnate and begin his visitation on earth.

Jesus and Mary lived the Life of the Divine Will on earth—Jesus by Nature and Mary by Gift. Redemption was accomplished by the Life, sufferings and death of Jesus, assisted in everything by his Mother.

With the Redemption man was placed in safety once again; but he was still far from where he had started in the Garden of Eden, where he lived in perfect unity with the Holy Trinity, sharing one same Life and Will.

Longing vehemently for the Father to grant once again the lost Gift of the Divine Will, Jesus prayed to his Father and our Father: "Thy Kingdom Come; Thy Will be done on earth as in Heaven!" He taught us all to pray that prayer, certain that the Father would one day give back to us the Kingdom of the Divine Will.

Non-Fiction

Let us close the topic of the Redemption with some additional points about Jesus' overwhelming interest in the Kingdom of the Divine Will:

1. When Jesus entered into his public life and began to preach, He said: "Do penance for the Kingdom of Heaven is at hand."

2. Jesus took the Apostles aside; and, in private, He taught them the mysteries of the Kingdom of God.

3. And Jesus sent the apostles to preach, bidding them to say: "The Kingdom of Heaven is at hand."

4. In the Gospel of St. Luke, Jesus speaks of the signs associated with the end times; and He says: "...when you see these things come to pass, know that the Kingdom of God is at hand."

5. At the Last Supper Jesus said: "In that day you shall know that I am in my Father and you in Me and I in you."

6. Also, at the Last Supper, Our Lord prayed to his Father: "That they may all be one as Thou, Father, in Me and I in Thee; that they may also be one in Us...I in them and Thou in me; that they may be made perfect in one..."

7. And Jesus once said in the Gospels: "...and there shall be one fold and one shepherd."

Suddenly and Unexpectedly

This kind of unity on earth can only happen when mankind has one will in common with one another and with God!

Now we will close this section on the Redemption with some reflections about Jesus' Agony in the Garden based upon the *"Book of Heaven"* by the Servant of God, Luisa Piccarreta.

During his Agony in the Garden of Gethsemane Jesus said; "Father, if it is possible, pass this chalice from Me; yet not my will but yours be done."

Jesus explained to Luisa that with those words He was not speaking of the chalice of his Passion but the chalice of man's human will that contained so much bitterness and vice that His own human will, united to the Divine, felt overwhelmed with repugnance and bitterness that He cried out to the Father, "If it is possible, let this chalice pass from Me!"

He further explained that all the evil in the world is due to the human will separated from the Divine Will and that seeing Himself covered with all the evil effects of the human will before his own Sanctity He experienced the feeling of dying and actually would have died had not the Divinity sustained Him.

Then He told Luisa that He said three times to his Father, "Not my will but yours be done." He did this in the name of everyone, begging the Father that the human will no longer be done on earth but only the Divine Will; and He besought the banishment of the human will so that the Father's Will would come to reign. And the thing most important to Him was to call to earth the "Your Will be done on earth as in Heaven."

With that Jesus constituted the time of the Reign of the Divine Will on earth as in Heaven. With his three beggings in the name of everyone, He successfully obtained from the Father, first, the coming of the Reign of the Divine Will, second, Its descent upon the earth, and, third, Its sovereign dominion as ruler.

Because Jesus' death on the Cross was imminent, He wanted to make a contract with his Heavenly Father so that his prime purpose for coming to the earth would be fulfilled, namely that the Divine Will take Its proper place of honor in mankind. The prime offense of man was his withdrawal from the Divine Will in the Garden of Eden. All other evils fall in the secondary order. The Divine Will always has primacy in all things, and, although Redemption and Its fruits have been seen before the realization of the effects of this contract with the Heavenly Father, it is in virtue of this contract that Jesus made with his Father during the Agony in the Garden that the Divine Will will have Its glorious reign on earth as in Heaven—the true purpose for the creation of man and the primary purpose of Jesus' coming to earth and being born in Bethlehem.

Jesus revealed to Luisa that in the mystery of his Will she was together with Him during his Agony in the Garden of Gethsemane and united with Him in crying to the Father, "Not my will but yours be done" because it was necessary that at least one human creature should render that contract valid.

VI. Summary: The Primary Purpose of everything, as much in Creation as in Redemption, is that man should live in the DIVINE WILL—the Father's Kingdom.

There is nothing that Jesus did that did not have as its primary purpose man taking possession of the Divine Will and Jesus taking possession of man's will. This was true both in the Fiat of Creation and in the Fiat of Redemption. The Sacraments that Jesus instituted and the Graces given to the saints have all been seeds and means toward the arrival of man's possession of the Divine Will.

Jesus told Luisa that God's ideal in Creation was the Kingdom of his Will in the souls of men, making mankind so many images of the Holy Trinity. Man withdrew from this ideal, but God has not abandoned his ideal, nor has Jesus set aside his prime purpose. He formed this

Kingdom first in his Immaculate Mother, and now after 2000 years of hearing the Our Father prayed, God has formed this Kingdom in Luisa, giving her all the teachings on how others can receive this great Kingdom and begin to live in the Divine Will once again as in the Garden of Eden.

Comment:

Even though now, in the year 2012, as the Kingdom is becoming better known and understood, the bloody battle between the human will and the Divine Will continues. But we have the beautiful hope that Jesus, Mary and Luisa are now experiencing from Heaven a new joy, because they see that the bloody battle between the human will and the Divine Will is entering its final phase; and, at long last, The Reign of the Divine Will is about to shine gloriously over all the earth! And this is none other than the fulfillment of Jesus' Prayer to his Father: "Thy Kingdom Come. Thy Will be done on earth as It is in Heaven"!

Postscript

Now let us review the great plan of God for mankind. Here, we must speak of the Three Fiats of God concerning humanity. The First Fiat of God is Creation, which is appropriated to the Father. The Second Fiat of God is Redemption, which is appropriated to the Son. And the Third Fiat of God is Sanctification of "Thy Will be done on Earth as in Heaven." This is appropriated to The Holy Spirit.

In the First Fiat of God, Creation, we have Adam and Eve who had the prime duty of maintaining themselves in the perfect state of Unity with the Trinity in which the Lord God had placed them. Adam and Eve possessed God. They possessed the Divine Will and were animated and directed by the Vital Principle of God Himself. When the TEST came to confirm them in this sublime, original state, Adam and Eve stopped loving God above all things. They chose to do their own will and withdrew from the Divine Will reigning in them.

At that point the human will began to reign on earth; and it still reigns to this very day, notwithstanding the Redemption and all the benefits of the Catholic Church.

The human will on its own, separated from unity with the Divine Will, is weak, inconstant, vacillating and prone to evil. It is the sole cause of all the evils of this earth.

Mankind was forced to wait 4000 years for the coming of the Redeemer, Jesus Christ, who not only redeemed us but regained for us the Lost Gift of the Divine Will. Because mankind was still in its infancy regarding spiritual things and incapable of properly understanding and using what is most noble, which is the Gift of the Divine Will, Divine Wisdom required another learning period of almost

2000 years. Therefore, Jesus taught us to pray for what most interested Him and which would most benefit us and which would most glorify his Father and our Father. He taught us the "Our Father" in which all Christianity is constantly beseeching the Father to grant once again what had been given to our first parents, Adam and Eve that the Divine Will be done in the very same manner as in Heaven.

So, in the Second Fiat of God, we have Jesus and Mary. Jesus possesses the Divine Will by virtue of his Divine Nature to which his Human Nature and Human Will are perfectly unified. Mary, the Mother and Queen of the Divine Will, was endowed with the Divine Will by gift at the moment of her Immaculate Conception. Mary's TEST was to never do her own will in anything, even in the good She might want to do, but to always let the Divine Will reign freely in Her, directing and animating all that She did.

Now, in God's Plan for man, comes the Third Fiat of God, the Reign of the Divine Will on earth as in Heaven. To bring about the fulfillment of this Eternal Decree, the Lord God was pleased to give us Luisa Piccarreta of Corato, Italy. In Luisa, God would work the prodigy of prodigies—the Divine Will reigning once again in mankind, as in the beginning. Luisa would be the Herald of the Divine Will, the Little Daughter of the Divine Will, the Teacher of the most Sublime Science found in the 36 glorious Volumes of the *"Book of Heaven"* which she obediently wrote during her long confinement to bed. This is why there is so much excitement in the air. This is why there is so much joy in the souls of good will, in spite of the immensity of the evil of our times.

What is the connection of The Fatima-Garabandal Reality with the coming Reign of the Divine Will?

1.   "The end of the times" made known during the Garabandal events corresponds with the "Third Renewal of the world" about which Jesus told Luisa Piccarreta. At Garabandal it is reported that Our Lady told Jacinta about a *"mysterious 'spiritual coming' of Christ."* This is in agreement with the insights of some of the Church Fathers and St. Bernard of Clairvaux, of which Pope John Paul II reminded us. This "spiritual coming of Christ" can certainly be accommodated to the understanding of "living Hosts" and the coming Reign of the Divine Will made known in the *"Book of Heaven."*

2.   The general confusion which Our Lady predicted at Garabandal corresponds to what Jesus told Luisa Piccarreta about the general confusion that would lead to the Third Renewal of the World.

3.   The predicted Chastisement mentioned at Garabandal corresponds to what Jesus told Luisa about the need for a Chastisement to cleanse the world to make it a proper place for His Kingdom to reign in souls.

4.   "Think about the Passion of Jesus" were the last words of the Second Formal Message at Garabandal. "The Hours of the Passion" by Luisa Piccarreta are possibly the best meditations ever written on the Passion of Jesus.

5.   The effects of the Warning and Miracle will dispose millions upon millions of people with a thirst for the knowledge of the Divine Will and Its Kingdom.

6.   It is also nice to know that St. Padre Pio spoke so well of Fatima, Garabandal and Luisa Piccarreta.

7.   All of the above and much more not reported in this book are manifestly the signs of the Third Renovation of the World made known in the *"Book of Heaven"* and reported in Chapter 11 of this book. The first renovation was by Water—The Deluge. The second renovation was by the Blood of Jesus Christ. The Third renovation is the coming Fire from Heaven to prepare the earth for the universal reign of the Father's Will.

Now, back to the present realities of 2012 as this book is being witten: The overly abundant signs of these times should be obvious to all: economic, social, moral, unusual disturbances of nature, etc., are crystal clear. Only the blind don't see them due to their pride, loss of faith, immodesty and all forms of impurity, greed, materialism, selfishness, divorce, violations of the sabbath, rebellion against legitimate authority, lying, cheating, loss of common sense, unjust judges, the many so obvious sins against nature and acceptance of them, which also include contraception, abortion, mercy killing, human cloning, unspeakable acts of violence, and on and on and on... Can our Creator let this go on and on? Will He continue to let the beautiful, innocent little children that He knits together in their mother's wombs be slaughtered physically before they see the light of day or be slaughtered spiritually if they are fortunate enough to survive the womb? The answer is obvious and certain.

Please understand: This book was originally intended for a very limited readership—those already aware of many of the things contained herein. However, while working on this book I kept getting the inspiration to share it with a broad readership, because all members of the human family have the same Father in Heaven, who is very concerned about all of us.

Chapter Eleven

The Three Eras of the World and the Three Renovations of Water, Blood, and Fire; then Comes the Kingdom of the Father and Its Glorious Reign on Earth

We learn in the entry of January 29, 1919 of Volume 12 of the glorious writings on the coming Reign of the Father's Will on earth, which are contained in the *"Book of Heaven"* by Luisa Piccarreta, the following:

At a certain point in every two thousand year period God has renewed the world. The first renewal occurred with the Deluge in the times of Noah, when there were only eight survivors. In the second two thousand, God sent his only-begotten Son to earth where He, as Jesus of Nazareth, manifested his Humanity, gave the world the Gospel of Redemption, and spilled his Blood on Calvary bringing about the second renewal. Now, at this present time in history, at the end of the third two thousand years, God is bringing about a third renewal, which no one can stop. This irrevocable renewal is in progress and will soon be experienced by man in great suffering and the apparent disappearance of the Church, followed by a marvelous intervention of Divine Mercy and a renewed orientation toward goodness during a "certain period of peace."

The reason for the general confusion and upheavals of our time is the manifestation of the unchangeable reality that the present society of humans is undergoing a purging which will culminate with Fire from Heaven and the destruction of a great part of humanity. But this will not happen before the Great Tribulation of Communism, which will be stopped only by an unprecedented, marvelous act of Divine Mercy— namely, the Universal Warning to all Mankind, and the "certain period of peace"* of a relatively short duration. Nevertheless, the ultimate purging of Fire from Heaven will certainly come, which will be followed by the predicted, long period of peace and the unimpeded, glorious and most happy Reign of the Father's Will on earth as in Heaven for those who survive. It will be the Sabbath Time of human history in which God will rest in souls and souls will rest in God.

(*The Tribulation of Communism and the Warning were made known by the Virgin Mary, the Queen of Prophets, at Garabandal and the relatively short, "certain period of peace" was made known at Fatima. The long, perfect period of peace is affirmed in the *Book of Heaven,* authored by Luisa Piccarreta.)

We learn in the entries of September 18 and October 2, 1938, of Volume 36—the last volume of the *"Book of Heaven,"* the following: God will make use of all means—love, graces, chastisements—to touch the hearts and minds of the people of our times in order to bring about the reign of the Father's Will on earth. "When it seems that all true goodness must die, it will resurge more beautiful and majestic." Nevertheless, this resurgence of goodness, beauty and majesty will have to follow a sea of fire in which the whole world will be enveloped, leaving only those survivors willed by God to live in the most happy Kingdom of the Father's Will that Jesus taught us to pray to come.

Let no one doubt or try to resist the coming of the Reign of the Divine Will for this is an infallible and uncancellable decree of Almighty God made in Eternity in the Consistory of the Most Holy Trinity. The Lord our God would have wanted to conquer man by way of Love, but human perfidy impedes Him from doing it. Therefore, He will use his Justice, sweeping the earth to remove all the harmful human beings, who, like poisonous plants poison the innocent plants.

From entry dated May 18, 1915, in Volume 11 of the *"Book of Heaven,"* we are consoled to know that God will take care of the souls and places where there are persons who live in the Divine Will. This demonstrates that even in these times of overwhelming sin and disorder, there are souls, even now, who have already begun to live interiorly the Life of Heaven—the Life of the Father's Will, which is the same Life that God Himself lives from Eternity to Eternity.

Finally, in entry of November 1, 1899, in Volume 3 of the *"Book of Heaven,"* its author was first shown the terrible condition of the Church and then was shown its glorious and beautiful condition after the purification, and she exclaimed: *"O happy days! After this, days of triumph and peace dawned; the face of the earth seemed to be renewed, and the pillar* regained its original honor and glory. O happy days, I salute you from afar! Days which will give great glory to my Church, and great honor to God her Head!"*

(*The pillar represented the Church supported by the relatively few but persecuted and faithful members who were supporting it during its time of trial.)

Understanding God in the Coming New Era

Souls will realize their own nothingness, the Majesty of God, and will pray and yearn for the universal reign of the Father's Will in souls, understanding the supreme greatness of this Gift. They will recognize the continuous act of the Father's Will operating in them by being their breath, movement, heartbeat, their very life. They will understand what it means to live in the Divine Will and that the Act of God in them transforms their own actions into the most beautiful and divine prodigies, which astonish even the angels in Heaven.

God gave to Adam the Gift of his Divine Will to possess and to live life in common with God even while on earth. He did this so that Adam could love God with a Divine Will and, therefore, Adam's love would not be mere human love but Divine Love.

This Gift to Adam of the Divine Will is what gave Adam his original likeness to God. And this Gift is given to the souls in Heaven, which enables them to do the Will of the Father in the manner proper to Heaven and no longer in the inferior way it is done on earth where the human will lacks its original powers from its unity with the Divine Will.

When the Lord's Prayer is fulfilled in the new Era, souls will possess and live in the Divine Will as do the souls in Heaven. Thus the fortunate souls who live in the new era will love God in the manner that He loves them. They will love God with Divine Love. But this is only one aspect of the prodigies and delights of life in the coming new era.

The Light of the Divine Will possesses great secrets to be known by those who want to live in this Light, because this Light of the Father's Will has the strength to dispose souls to understand and live these divine secrets. This

Suddenly and Unexpectedly

Light will not only dispose souls to live these divine secrets but also to understand Him, the Supreme Being, who will be delighted with the most pleasing companionship of the souls who understand Him.

These souls will come to understand that living in the Divine Will was the purpose of Creation and that the primary purpose of Redemption was the recovery of this greatest of Gifts, which Jesus accomplished secretly during his hidden life in Nazareth, before entering his public life and then shedding His blood for our salvation. Shortly before the time of His crucifixion, Jesus taught the Apostles the Lord's Prayer, because it was so important to Him that the Father should appoint a time for the restoration of His Kingdom so that It could be possessed and lived in once again as it was in the beginning in the Garden of Eden.

That glorious and happy time is coming in the new era ahead for those who survive the pains and sufferings of the Third Renewal of the World, mentioned earlier, which has already begun and will be experienced more dramatically in the days ahead.

By having the Father's Kingdom within them, souls will have within them the Father Himself. They will have within them the One who created the sun, the stars, the galaxies. They will have within them the Father's Son, Jesus, who redeemed them, and they will have within them the Holy Spirit, who comforts them and sanctifies them.

When the Father's Will wants to speak, it looks to see if there is the space in the soul that the gift of Its word can occupy. In creating man, God gave him His greatest and most precious Gift—the Father's Will, as depository in him. This enabled the Holy Trinity to speak to man about the wonderful surprises and immense gifts that the Father's Kingdom contains.

When Adam sinned by disobedience to a simple command, he withdrew from the Father's Will and lost the Father's Kingdom that had been reigning in his soul. As a result, all humanity was deprived of the inheritance of man's original state and possession of the Fathers' Kingdom and the exalted life of living in the Divine Will as in Heaven.

Adam's own human will that had formerly been saturated with the life, beauty and holiness of the Divine Will was left bereft of these wonders. He became weak, vacillating and prone to evil as did Eve and all future generations, with the sole exception of the woman who was specially created to have the exalted dignity of becoming the Mother of the Son of God, who assumed human nature in her most pure womb. And this has been the foremost human problem ever since. All the evil on earth is the result of the human will separating from the Divine Will with Adam's sin. If Adam had not sinned there never would have been evil on earth.

Now, with the third renovation of the world presently underway and which will eventually reach its climax, Our Father in Heaven will grant the Prayer of his Son. The Father's Kingdom will be given to the survivors of this renovation, and at long last God will have what He has always wanted. The time will come when the Kingdom of the Father will reign in souls all over the world, and with this reign of the Father's Kingdom all sin and evil will be banished from the earth as Jesus asked in his Prayer, "deliver us from evil."

With this little introduction to the Reign of the Father's Will on earth as in Heaven, it might to be worth a look at the website: **comingofthekingdom.com.** There, one will find information that leads to more knowledge about this exceedingly great event that has already begun its way in souls even now, in preparation for the time when others will be disposed, following the terrible coming events of the renovation of the world reported in this book.

Concerning the *"Book of Heaven"* and its author:

In the mysterious Wisdom of God, before which we must all bow, it has come to be that the knowledge required for life in the Father's Kingdom on earth, destined for these times, has already been communicated from Heaven. Divine Wisdom has chosen to make this knowledge known to the Church through a very little soul of limited education, who was confined to bed for 64 years in the small Italian town of Corato, located not far from the port city of Bari on the Adriatic Sea.

For a period of 40 of the years of her confinement to bed, the Servant of God Luisa Piccarreta (1865-1947), was placed under obedience by her confessors to write in her diaries everything that Jesus made known to her about the Father's Kingdom and Its coming to reign in the souls of men. Her most notable confessor was St. Hannibal Di Francia, founder of the Rogationist Fathers of the Sacred Heart.

With only a first-grade education, Luisa Piccarreta wrote in her diaries the most sublime mysteries of God and his purpose for creating man, ever known. To these writings, destined to transform the face of the earth, Our Lord gave this title: ***"The Kingdom of the Fiat in the Midst of Creatures - Book of Heaven - the Call to the Creature to return to the Order, the Place, and the Purpose for which he was Created by God."***

[The word, "Fiat," refers to the Divine Will. The use of the word, "Creatures," refers to human beings created by God.]

The *"Book of Heaven"* consists of 36 Volumes written between February 28, 1899 and December 28, 1938.. Thirty-four of the 36 Volumes were placed in a special archive of the Vatican in 1938 and were photocopied in 1996 by a team of four priests and two persons of the laity and presented to the custody of the Archbishop of Trani, Italy, who has legal title to these writings. The other two Volumes, located in another place, were also photographed separately and also presented to the custody of the Archbishop of Trani. The Original Volumes are still in the special Vatican archive and are the subject of special ecclesial attention and care as this book is being written. The other two original volumes are apparently still in another place known to the Church.

Over a period of many years and at different times, seven Church-appointed priest theologians have given their approvals to these writings, without necessarily under-standing every mystery of the Divine Will contained in them.

Without going into the details here, the contents of the *"Book of Heaven"* have had an intricate history of limited diffusion to date. The author of this book, *"Suddenly and Unexpectedly..."*, by the grace of God, has had the opportunity to study these celestial writings for almost 40 years to date. The organization that the author leads, The Luisa Piccarreta Center for the Divine Will, Inc., provides considerable literature and other information about the now beginning Reign of the Father's Will, based on the *"Book of Heaven"*, including legitimate English versions of some of its 36 Volumes. The website associated with this Center is ***comingofthekingdom.com.***

———

Appendix

The Phenomenon of Fr. Stefano Gobbi

Fr. Stephano Gobbi (1930-2011) from the Province of Como, Italy, began a movement named, *"The Marian Movement of Priests,"* within the Catholic Church in 1972 following an experience he had while visiting Fatima, Portugal, in May of 1972. The experience he had was that of a locution from Mary, the Mother of Jesus. A locution is not an apparition but an interior voice, which speaks to the soul and is recognized by the person who hears that voice and is made to understand whose voice is being heard. For the next 39 years until his death, Fr. Gobbi traveled all over the world speaking to Cardinals, Bishops, Priests and laity, sharing with them what the Virgin Mary was continually telling him about our times. Here is part of one of the hundreds of messages She gave to Fr. Gobbi, recorded in the book, *"To the Priests–Our Lady's Beloved Sons."*

Suddenly and Unexpectedly

Why Am I Still Weeping? *(September 15, 1987 in Akita, Japan)*

Why am I still weeping?

I am weeping** because humanity is not accepting my motherly invitation to conversion and to its return to the Lord. It is continuing to run with obstinacy along the road of rebellion against God and against his Law of love. The Lord is openly denied, outraged and blasphemed. Your heavenly Mother is publicly despised and held up for ridicule. My extraordinary requests are not being accepted; the signs of my immense sorrow which I am giving are not believed.

Your neighbor is not loved: every day attacks are made upon his life and his goods. Man is becoming ever more corrupt, godless, wicked and cruel. A **chastisement worse than the flood** is about to come upon this poor and perverted humanity. Fire will descend from heaven, and this will be the sign that the justice of God has as of now fixed the hour of his great manifestation.

I am weeping because the Church is continuing along the road of division, of loss of the true faith, of apostasy and of errors which are being spread more and more without anyone offering opposition to them. Even now, that which I predicted at Fatima and that which I have revealed here in the third message confided to a little daughter* of mine are in the process of being accomplished. [*Sr.Agnes Sasagawa of Akita, Japan]

I am weeping because, in great numbers, the souls of my children are being lost and going to hell.

I am weeping because too few are those who accede to my request to pray, to make reparation, to suffer and to offer.

I am weeping because I have spoken to you and have not been listened to; I have given you miraculous signs, and I have not been believed; I have manifested myself to you in a strong and continuous way, but you have not opened the doors of your hearts to me.

At least you, my beloved ones and children consecrated to my Immaculate Heart, little remnant which Jesus is guarding jealously in the secure enclosure of his divine love, hearken to and accept this sorrowful request of mine which, from this place, I address again today to all the nations of the earth. Prepare yourselves to receive Christ in the splendor of his glory, because the great day of the Lord has even now arrived.

(Note: The last sentence can be interpreted in a way consistent with Christ's hidden coming in the Reign of the Divine Will.)

In biblical times, God used the prophets to warn His people when their transgressions against the law were reaching the breaking point. In our time, it is the Blessed Virgin, Queen of Prophets, who fulfills that role. At Fatima she foretold the Second World War and the spread of atheistic communism if the world did not change. At Garabandal, in other places and by other means She warns of the greatest cataclysm in human history since the deluge if mankind does not reform.

**Mary's weeping has been continuously demonstrated all over the world for the past 3-4 decades through the tears flowing from her images (paintings, statues and other means). This display of the grave, maternal concern for her children on earth, though often in the news, is almost entirely ignored or ridiculed, in spite of the lab tests that the tears are almost always proven to be human tears or even human blood in some cases.

The December 1957 Interview:
Fr. Augustin Fuentes with Lucia of Fatima

On December 26, 1957, Father Augustin Fuentes interviewed Sister Lucia at her convent in Coimbra, Portugal. Later, with an imprimatur and the approbation of the Bishop of Fatima, Father Fuentes published the following revelations concerning the Third Secret, revealed to him by Sister Lucia during that interview. She obviously thought that the Third Secret would be made public in 1960, but it wasn't. Sister Lucia's apprehension concerning the world's future—for the "imminent punishment from Heaven"—is both striking and revealing.

Extract of that Interview with Sister Lucia:

"Father, the Most Holy Virgin is very sad because no one has paid any attention to Her message, neither the good nor the bad. The good continue on their way but without giving any importance to Her message. The bad, not seeing the punishment of God actually falling upon them, continue their life of sin without even caring about the message. But believe me, Father, God will chastise the world and this will be in a terrible manner. *The punishment from Heaven is imminent.*

"Father, how much time is there before 1960 arrives? It will be very sad for everyone, not one person will rejoice at all if beforehand the world does not pray and do penance. *I am not able to give any other details because it is still a secret. . .*

"This is the third part of the Message of Our Lady, which will remain secret until 1960.

"Tell them, Father, that many times the most Holy Virgin told my cousins Francisco and Jacinta, as well as myself, that many nations will disappear from the face of the earth. She said that Russia will be the instrument of chastisement chosen by

Suddenly and Unexpectedly

Heaven to punish the whole world if we do not beforehand obtain the conversion of that poor nation.

"Father, the devil is in the mood for engaging in a decisive battle against the Blessed Virgin. And the devil knows what it is that most offends God and which in a short space of time will gain for him the greatest number of souls. *Thus, the devil does everything to overcome souls consecrated to God, because in this way, the devil will succeed in leaving the souls of the faithful abandoned by their leaders, thereby the more easily will he seize them.*

"That which afflicts the Immaculate Heart of Mary and the Heart of Jesus is the fall of religious and priestly souls. The devil knows that *religious and priests who fall away from their beautiful vocation drag numerous souls to hell. ...* The devil wishes to take possession of consecrated souls. He tries to corrupt them in order to *lull to sleep the souls of lay people and thereby lead them to final impenitence.*"

The following article by Fr. Jim Anderson, is included in this book with his permission. It provides a well researched evaluation of the apparent inconsistencies of understanding concerning whether or not the consecration of Russia to the Immaculate Heart of Mary has been accomplished according to the requests of Our Lady and Our Lord.

155

From Fatima to Russia
Time is Growing Short

by Fr. Jim Anderson, M.S.A.

In the Vatican's "The Message of Fatima" published in July 2000, Cardinal Tarciscio Bertone, SDB, then Secretary of the Congregation for the Doctrine of the Faith, asserted that *"any further discussion or request"* for the consecration of Russia to the Immaculate Heart of Mary by the Holy Father and his Bishops *"is without basis"* because *"Sister Lucia personally confirmed that this solemn and universal act of consecration"* had already been accomplished by Pope John Paul II. Bertone's only authority for such a "game changing" assertion were two typed lines from a letter he claimed to have been written by Sister Lucia on 8 November 1989 stating that: *"Yes it has been done just as Our Lady asked, on 25 March 1984."*

But is it probable that Sister Lucia, after 60 years of urgently proclaiming to a succession of pontiffs the Blessed Mother's request that the Holy Father order his Bishops to join him in solemnly consecrating Russia to her Immaculate Heart, would then state in 1989 that John Paul II's consecration of the world *"corresponded to what Our Lady wished?"* Considering Lucia's well known mind-set for these 60 years this writer must concur with those scholars who conclude that Sister Lucia could not in conscience have composed such a letter.

Suddenly and Unexpectedly

The credibility of Bertone's claim is further weakened by the failure to include for readers of this document a fuller text of the letter, its addressee, or the signature of the author. It is at least disproportionate to base such a grave claim on such thin evidence. Moreover, there is a fatal contradiction to the possibility that Sister Lucia wrote the letter.

After the death of Sister Lucia's eldest sister, Senhora Maria dos Anjos, the then Rector of the Sanctuary of Fatima, the Rev. Msgr. Luciano Guerra, had asked Sister Lucia to complete her childhood recollections of her family, especially of her father. Sister Lucia gladly complied, writing as always in her own hand a Fifth Memoir, which begins with a letter to Msgr. Guerra, dated 12 February 1989. Sister Lucia there refers to Msgr. Guerra's letter to her of 23 November 1988 requesting the further recollections, and to a previous questionnaire Guerra had sent to her via her Provincial, Fr. Jeremias Carlos Vechina on 31 October 1986, requesting a prompt response, which her community duties prevented. Two years later a new provincial, Fr. Pedro Ferreira, believing the work to be for the glory of God, advised her not to delay longer. She then explained to Msgr. Guerra: *believing this to be the will of God, and because it is what Your Reverence needs more speedily, I am going to begin by describing the portrait of my father, trusting in the material protection of Our Lady.*

The responses to your questionnaire will be made afterwards, but, for now, I must say that to some - those referring to the Apparitions - I cannot reply without authorization from the Holy See, unless you would like to ask for this permission and obtain it. Otherwise, I will go ahead, leaving those questions blank. [Emphasis added]

157

Is it, likewise, probable that after explaining in her handwritten letter to Msgr. Guerra on 12 February 1989 that she could not reply to questions *"referring to the Apparitions without authorization from the Holy See,"* that on 8 November 1989 Sister Lucia would type the letter cited by Archbishop Bertone? Given Sister Lucia's personal moral integrity and her devotion to Our Lady and her messages, it is more than improbable; it is unthinkable that she would confirm that the 25 March 1984 consecration of the world corresponded to what Our Lady had asked in her apparition on 13 July 1917 at Fatima.

Moreover, it is not clear from Archbishop Bertone's text that the 8 November 1989 letter, whether typewritten by Sister Lucia or not, refers to the consecration of Russia proposed by Our Lady at Fatima. The consecration of the world to the Immaculate Heart of Mary is important and pleasing to Heaven and has been the cause of significant blessings in the past. But the promise of Our Lady of Fatima that Russia would be converted and that there would be world peace is conditioned on our Pontiff heeding her request for the consecration of Russia and the First Saturday devotions of reparation. There were, in fact, two distinct requests and two distinct promises by Heaven. Assuming for argument that the 8 November 1989 letter was typewritten by Sister Lucia, it is most probable that the seer would have been confirming only that a second and different request, that the Holy Father consecrate the world to the Immaculate Heart of Mary, had been accomplished as Heaven wished. This conclusion follows from the following historical sequence.

Suddenly and Unexpectedly

On 1 August 1935 Our Lord asked another Portuguese seer, Alexandrina Maria da Costa, to write to the Holy Father asking him to consecrate the world to the Immaculate Heart of Mary. Her Jesuit confessor, Father Pinho, forwarded her letter to Pius XI through Cardinal Eugenio Pacelli on 11 September 1936. Pacelli instigated an investigation of the seer by the Holy Office, involving the Portuguese authorities. Coincidentally, Fr. Pinho preached a retreat to the Portuguese Bishops at Fatima in June 1938. Since previous requests for the consecration of Russia had resulted in obstinate silence from Rome, and since the world was once more rapidly descending into chaos, the Portuguese Bishops sent a collective request to the pontiff that he consecrate the world to the Immaculate Heart of Mary. They urged that the protection God had given to Portugal in response to their having consecrated that country to the Immaculate Heart of Mary could be extended to the whole world by a similar consecration by the Holy Father. Pius XI, however, remained silent.

Efforts by Sister Lucia's spiritual directors to obtain the consecration of Russia by the Holy Father with his Bishops seemed futile by the fall of 1940. Impelled by the immense dangers threatening the world they hoped to obtain instead the Holy Father's consecration of the world with a special mention of Russia. They ordered her to write to the Holy Father to ask for this. On 22 October 1940 Sister Lucia spent two hours in prayer before the Blessed Sacrament and received this new promise from Our Lord:

His Holiness will obtain an abbreviation of these days of tribulation [World War II] if he takes heed of My

159

wishes by promulgating the Act of Consecration of the whole world to the Immaculate Heart of Mary, with a special mention of Russia.

On 2 December 1940 Sister Lucia wrote a letter from Tuy, Spain, to his holiness Pius XII that had been severely edited by Bishop da Silva of Leiria-Fatima, recalling the history of Our Lady's requests at Fatima and at Tuy:

I come, Most Holy Father, to renew a request that has already been brought to you several times. The request, Most Holy Father, is from Our Lord and Our Good Mother in Heaven.

In 1917, in the portion of the apparitions that we have designated 'the secret,' the Blessed Virgin revealed the end of the war that was then afflicting Europe, and predicted another forthcoming, saying that to prevent it She would come and ask for the consecration of Russia to Her Immaculate Heart as well as the Communion of reparation on the First Saturday [of the month]. She promised peace and the conversion of that nation if Her request was attended to. She announced that otherwise this nation would spread her errors throughout the world, and there would be wars, persecution of the Holy Church, martyrdom of many Christians, several persecutions and sufferings reserved for Your Holiness, and the annihilation of several nations

Most Holy Father, this remained a secret until 1926 according to the express will of Our Lady.

Suddenly and Unexpectedly

In 1929, through another apparition, Our Lady asked for the consecration of Russia to Her Immaculate Heart, promising its conversion through this means and the hindering of the propagation of its errors.

Sometime afterwards I told my confessor of the request of Our Lady. He employed certain means to fulfill it by making it known to His Holiness Pius XI.

In several intimate communications Our Lord has not stopped insisting on this request, **promising lately, to shorten the days of tribulation with which He has determined to punish the nations for their crimes, through war, famine and several persecutions of the Holy Church and Your Holiness, if you will consecrate the world to the Immaculate Heart of Mary, with a special mention of Russia, and order that all the bishops of the world do the same in union with Your Holiness.**

Most Holy Father, if in the union of my soul with God I have not been deceived, Our Lord promises a special protection to our country **in this war,** *due to the consecration of the nation, by the Portuguese Prelates, to the Immaculate Heart of Mary; as proof of the graces that would have been granted to other nations, had they also consecrated themselves to Her.* [Emphasis added]

Noted Fatima scholars Fr. Joaquin Maria Alonso, C.M.F. and Frere Michel de la Sainte Trinite, C.R.C. concur that at Fatima in 1917 and at Tuy in 1929 God asked through Mary for the consecration of Russia by the Holy Father with his Bishops, promising in return the conversion of Russia and world peace. Failing that, on 22 October 1940 *"Heaven acceded to the desires of Sister Lucia's superiors, to see the consecration of the world with a special mention of Russia brought about. It is the Lord Himself who suggests such an act."* But for this latter consecration the Lord promised not the conversion of Russia and world peace, but only the abbreviation of the tribulation of World War II.

Finally, on 31 October 1942 Pius XII did so consecrate the world. Immediately thereafter the tide of battle turned on several fronts, including Stalingrad in Russia and El Alamein in North Africa, undoubtedly abbreviating the tribulation of World War II. But Sister Lucia then made no claim that such consecration of the world had been made just as Our Lady had proposed at Fatima in 1917 and requested with Jesus at Tuy in 1929 because that was clearly not the case! On 28 February 1943 Lucia wrote to her frequent correspondent, Bishop Manuel Ferreira da Silva, titular Bishop of Gurza: *"The Good Lord has already shown me His contentment with the act performed by the Holy Father and several bishops, although it was incomplete according to His desire. In return He promises to end the war soon. The conversion of Russia is not for now."* Indeed, Russia was not converted and a period of peace was not granted to the world. On the contrary, Russia spread her errors throughout the world. A dangerous cold war and a series of deadly hot wars impoverished, enslaved, and killed tens of thousands of human beings. An "Iron Curtain" divided Europe. Atheism, persecution of the Church, the terror, the Gulag, and a total suppression of freedom in communist eastern European nations and in communist Southeast Asian and Asian nations followed.

Suddenly and Unexpectedly

Likewise, the consecration of the world by John Paul II on 25 March 1984 has not resulted in either the conversion of Russia or in world peace, although there is much evidence that Blessed John Paul's act did bring many blessings to this troubled world. On 13 May 1984 a fire broke out within the Soviet naval arsenal at Severomorsk on the North Sea resulting in a series of explosions that on 17 May utterly demolished the facility. Until then the Soviet leadership had seriously considered a pre-emptive nuclear attack on the NATO allies during the Euro missile Crisis. Antonio Socci reports that according to military historian Alberto Leoni: *"Without that missile apparatus that controlled the North Sea the USSR did not have any hope of victory. For this reason the military option was canceled."* Commenting on this event, and on John Paul's faith that the liberation of Poland was a beneficial intervention of the Madonna, Sister Lucia, being questioned by the Italian journal *"Thirty Days"* declared: *"I am completely in accord with what the Holy Father has said ... I believe this involves an action of God in the world, to liberate it from the danger of an atomic war that could destroy it, and an insistent call to all of humanity for a more lively faith."* Yet the demise of the Berlin Wall and the apparent political restructuring of the former Soviet Union and Eastern Europe is neither the conversion of Russia nor the period of world peace promised at Fatima. So to which of these two separate and distinct consecrations requested by Heaven does the typewritten letter of November 8, 1989 proffered by Cardinal Bertone as from Sister Lucia refer?

From the first Sister Lucia has been adamant that at Fatima the Holy Mother had asked for the consecration of the country of Russia alone, not the world. The Lord had explained to her that He would not convert Russia without such consecration: *"Because I want My whole Church to acknowledge that consecration as a triumph of the Immaculate Heart of Mary."* However, it appears that John Paul II believed that he could not consecrate Russia alone, but that heaven would be satisfied that he had done all that could be done in the practical circumstances. On 1 August 1984 John Paul II told Father Pierre Caillon, a retired philosophy professor who had studied the issue of the Consecration of Russia for years, that *"the consecration is done. . . we cannot Consecrate Russia apart by itself. We have consecrated all of the nations and we have added a special mention for the nation which Our Lady was expecting the consecration."*

Several conclusions follow from these facts:

(1) Sister Lucia knew that the consecration of Russia apart by itself was a condition of the conversion of Russia and world peace.

(2) Lucia understood Jesus' reason why He would not convert Russia without the distinct consecration of Russia apart from a general consecration of all countries: ***"Because I want My whole Church to acknowledge that consecration as a triumph of the Immaculate Heart of Mary."*** [Emphasis added.] For Lucia to have composed the 9 November 1989 typewritten letter would have contradicted what she knew to be the will of God.

(3) Sister Lucia could not have stated that the 25 March 1984 consecration of the world fully satisfied

Heaven's condition for the Conversion of Russia and world peace given during the 13 July 1917 apparition at Fatima, that the Holy Father with his Bishops solemnly consecrate Russia to the Immaculate Heart, without disobeying the Vatican order that she not discuss the apparitions without explicit permission.

(4) Whoever composed the November 8, 1989 type-written letter was unaware of the two different requests and promises for the consecration of Russia and the consecration of the World to the Immaculate Heart of Mary, rendering its assertion, and that of Cardinal Bertone, ambiguous at best.

It follows from each of these conclusions that the Vatican's "The Message of Fatima" erred in claiming that Sister Lucia wrote the November 8, 1989 letter asserting that Heaven had accepted the 25 March 1984 consecration of the world as fully complying with the 13 July 1917 promises made at Fatima. Why is this error important to us? It remains to briefly consider the tragic consequences for the Church and the world if this claim of Cardinal Bertone continues to be believed by the leaders of the Church and the faithful.

Since 1960 the Vatican's *Ostpolitik* and diplomatic and social justice initiatives, like those proclaimed by John XXIII in *Pacem in Terris,* have failed to accomplish the conversion of Russia, to bring peace to the world, or any significant betterment in human behavior that would evidence the conversion of sinners' hearts and minds to Christ. And while significant blessings in the form of reductions of the tribulation of WWII and the Cold War have been obtained by the consecrations of the world to the Immaculate Heart by both Pius XII and John Paul II, *"how much greater would they have been had the Madonna been heeded?"*

Cardinal Bertone's assertion in "The Message of Fatima" that Sister Lucia confirmed that the 1984 consecration of the world satisfied heaven has succeeded in continuing the ongoing suppression of Mary's 1917 requests at Fatima for the Consecration of Russia and the First Saturday reparatory devotions since its publication in July of 2000. But that period has seen, *inter alia,* the 9-11 destruction of the World Trade Center towers in New York City, ongoing tension between the Koreas, costly destructive wars in Iraq, Afghanistan, Libya, Syria, and Egypt, a real threat of nuclear war between Israel and its allies and Iran and its allies, the ongoing genocide of Sudanese and Nigerian Catholics by Muslim militias, increasing military competition between the United States and Communist China, a quiet but significant buildup of Russian nuclear weapons, and growing mutual mistrust between Russia and China and the West. Thus it is ludicrous to maintain that the consecration of Russia has been done as asked by Heaven at Fatima, or that the *Ostpolitik* of the Vatican or its diplomatic efforts in the United Nations have achieved world peace. Rather, the world has experienced continual war. It appears to this writer that there is no time for business as usual by the Church as if there were endless centuries to work for Christ. Heaven has given the Holy Father and his Bishops specific orders at Fatima; they are not optional!

Jesus told Peter: *"Put out into the deep and lower your nets for a catch."* Peter replied: *"Master, we toiled all night and took nothing! But at your word I will let down the nets."*

Benedict is Peter! He has all the authority he needs from Jesus, alone. He can avoid alarming the Russians or offending the Orthodox by ordering his Bishops to join him in consecrating a series of countries including Russia one by one, each by itself alone, to the Immaculate Heart of Mary on the 13th day of every month. He can personally lead the Church in the First Saturday reparatory devotions to the Immaculate Heart of Mary. If Benedict does that he will lead the Church to victory over Lucifer as David led Israel to victory over Goliath and the Philistines. If he will not, then the world is poised to experience the Triumph of the Immaculate Heart of Mary, the conversion of Russia and a period of world peace only after the further chastisements prophesied by the Blessed Mother after Sister Lucia was forbidden to speak on the apparitions without Vatican approval in 1960.

From 1961 to 1971 Mary appeared to four children at Garabandal, Spain calling all to repentance and warning of punishment by a horrific chastisement should the world remain rebellious. Mary revealed to Saint Padre Pio that the Garabandal apparitions were true. On 13 October 1973 at Akita, Japan the Blessed Mother prophesied to Sister Agnes Sasagawa intense persecution of and conflict within the Church and an unimaginable chastisement if the world did not repent. The prophesies at Akita are approved by the Church and in 1998 were reliably confirmed to be *"an extension of"* and *"essentially the same"* as the message of Fatima, by then Cardinal Joseph Ratzinger.

We in the Church must daily fast and pray to support Pope Benedict XVI as he prayerfully contemplates the promises and warnings of the three parts of the Message of Fatima within the prophetic context of Garabandal and Akita, and to defeat his enemies, visible and invisible, who work against him, within and without Christ's Church!

Maranatha! Come, Lord Jesus!

Note: The many sources of reference for Fr. Anderson's article are contained in the endnotes of the original article.

Commentary: It is true that the request of Mary, and of Our Lord, have not been carried out regarding Russia. Some earlier popes are more to be blamed, and by certain actions (and other factors) have made it very difficult for recent popes. Example: Pope John Paul II said: "My hands are tied."

———————

A Few Words about the Catholic Church

The Church that Jesus founded was to be available to everyone. It was essentially universal or catholic, open to all. That is why the Church He founded is called the Catholic Church, and He is its Head. He ascended to his Father in Heaven with His spiritualized, glorified, natural body forty days after his resurrection. He appointed the apostle and bishop, Peter, to represent Him on earth as head of His universal Catholic Church until Peter's own death, to be succeeded by another bishop elected by fellow bishops, and so on until the end of Time. Jesus, referring to St. Peter and his successors said, "That thou art Peter; and upon this rock I will build my church, and the gates of hell shall not prevail against it. And I will give to thee the keys of the kingdom of heaven. And whatsoever thou shalt

Suddenly and Unexpectedly

bind upon earth, it shall be bound also in heaven: and whatsoever thou shalt loose upon earth, it shall be loosed also in heaven." (Mt: 16, 18-19)

Jesus said to his disciples: "It needs be that scandals should come: but woe to him through whom they come." (Lk: 17,1)

Jesus also said, "Behold I am with you all days, even to the consummation of the world."(Mt: 28,20)

We are now in the time of the foretold, great apostasy, and the last great battle. This last great battle is a battle between Satan with his deceiving, murderous agents on one side and the Woman and her seed on the other. Mary is the Woman, and her seed are those who are obedient and faithful to her Son, Jesus.

As this last great battle continues, the forces of evil will win many more skirmishes, giving the impression that their side is the winning side. Things will arrive to the extreme point that the Catholic Church will seem to disappear. Then suddenly, almost instantaneously, everything will change. The Woman and her seed, through their intercession and favor with the Most High, will defeat the forces of evil, and victory will be with those who have persevered with faith in their Lord—the Son of God—Jesus. And then, after a certain period of peace and another time of trial, the universal extension of the Father's Kingdom—the Kingdom of the Divine Will—will permeate the resurrected Catholic

169

Church, having entered its Glorified State. The face of the earth will be transformed and there will be One Fold and One Shepherd, and a long period of tranquility. One Will—the Divine Will—will reign and operate in the souls of men, just as It does in Heaven. All will be peace, harmony, and happiness.

But for now a few leaders, including some bishops and priests in the United States of America and elsewhere, are telling those in their care to prepare for suffering and martyrdom. The imminent tribulation, which will come "suddenly and unexpectedly" will be horrible beyond our imagination. Even most of those who already sense pending trouble and are warning others of the dire consequences of the growing economic and social chaos and are giving advice on how to survive, or even profit from them, have no idea what is coming.

May those who have read these pages avoid the mistakes of the people who lived nonchalantly in the days of Noah. For what does it profit a man to gain the whole world and suffer the loss of his soul. In the end, the only successful persons are those who enjoy the unending happiness of eternity with their Creator. Most sorrowfully, all others will be miserable, unsuccessful, everlasting losers.

> There shall be weeping and gnashing of teeth, when you shall see Abraham and Isaac and Jacob, and all the prophets, in the Kingdom of God, and you yourselves thrust out. (Lk 13: 28)

Vision of Pope Pius IX (1878)

"Since the whole world is against God and His Church, it is evident that He has reserved the victory over His enemies to Himself. This will be more obvious when it is considered that the root of all our present evils is to be found in the fact that those with talents and vigor crave earthly pleasures, and not only desert God but repudiate Him altogether.

"Thus it appears they cannot be brought back in any other way except through an act that cannot be ascribed to any secondary agency, and thus all will be forced to look to the supernatural...

"There will come a great wonder, which will fill the world with astonishment. This wonder will be preceded by the triumph of revolution. The church will suffer exceedingly. Her servants and her chieftain will be mocked, scourged, and martyred."

Author's Comment: All that is written in this book is about the present and continuing third renewal of the world so that it will be purified and prepared to be a fit place for the Reign of the Father's Will on earth as in Heaven, which will be a time of incalculable happiness.

Bibliography

Garabandal

She went in Haste to the Mountain by Fr. Eusebio Garcia de Pesquera O.F.M., Cap.

The Village Speaks by Ramon Pérez

Garabandal by Jacques Serre and Beatrix Caux

Garabandal Journal Magazine by Barry Hanratty

Conversations with journalist-author, Albrecht Weber

The Internet

Fatima

The Internet (Note: There is also an abundance of books and other literature about Fatima)

The Kingdom of the Father's Will on earth as in Heaven

The Book of Heaven by Luisa Piccarreta

Bible Quotes

Douay-Rheims Version - (TAN Books and Publishers)

Revised Standard Version – (Ignatius Press)

Private translation of part of one quote

———————

About the Author

T. Michael Fahy, had an unusual experience while working at the offices of a major oil company, in New York, NY, at the age of 31. Soon after his unusual experience, he left that company in New York and began to follow the lead indicated by that experience. Now, 42 years later, having devoted all those years to constant discovery and teaching what has been made known to him by following that lead, the author realizes that the time has arrived to share with his brothers and sisters in the human race what he has learned, in this very unique book—before it is too late.

Quick Reference to the Major Events Ahead

Undoubtedly, economic, military, and other social upheavals will continue, but the sequence of the most important and serious events in this time of the "Third renovation of the world" are:

1. The *sudden and unexpected* tribulation of communism led by Russia and the horrifying effects described in this book and elsewhere.

2. The *sudden and unexpected* Divine Warning to all humanity, which stops the communist tribulation and corrects the conscience of the world.

3. The Great Miracle at Garabandal during which we will see the Glory of God.

4. The future Chastisement of Fire from Heaven

5. The long period of peace of the Father's Kingdom on earth as in Heaven.

173

Made in the USA
Charleston, SC
16 May 2013